MS MADNESS!

A "Giggle More, Cry Less"
Story of Multiple Sclerosis

by

Yvonne deSousa

Laughter is the best medicine !

Yvonne deSousa 😊
8/14

MS Madness, Published February, 2014

Editorial and Proofreading Services: Aileen McDonough and Karen Grennan

Interior Layout and Cover Design: Dianne Rux Leonetti - D'ziner Graphics

Photo Credits: Cover image by Randy Jennings. Author photo taken by Megan O'Leary

Published by SDP Publishing,
an imprint of SDP Publishing Solutions, LLC.

For more information about this book contact Lisa Akoury-Ross by email at lross@SDPPublishing.com.

ISBN-13 (print): 978-0-9899723-6-9
e-ISBN-13 (ebook): 978-0-9911597-4-1

Library of Congress Control Number: 2013951940

Printed in the United States of America

Dedication

My mom likes to say that "friends are the family you choose." The words move me. All of my life, I have been incredibly fortunate to hold dear many loyal and supportive friends. Even in moments when you feel like you have nothing, if you have a friend you can call on you are blessed.

This book is dedicated to all of my dear friends, but especially those living with multiple sclerosis. Topping that list is my friend and sister Laurie, who had to learn how to cope with this illness without any medical guidance from the family. When it was my time to have questions, I only had to reach out and ask her. She had been there already and was able and willing to pave the way, shots, Canadian crutch, leg brace, cooling vest, and all.

As a thank you to all of the above wonderful people, and far too many others I have yet to meet, a portion of the proceeds from the sale of this book will be donated to organizations dedicated to helping those living with chronic illness and finding a cure for multiple sclerosis.

Note: While this story is completely true, some names of people mentioned have been changed just in case their memories differ from the brain fog I may have been having when I wrote the stories that describe events pertaining to them.

Table of Contents

Prologue

*"A cheerful heart is good medicine,
but a crushed spirit dries up the bones."*
— Proverbs 17:22 NIV

"I'm not going to lie to you. MS sucks. You and I are going to become good friends," said a woman I had met only twenty-three minutes before, in a place I had never been, seven days before Christmas. She had a lot of letters and titles after her name and many fancy certificates on her wall. And she looked very wise. But all I thought was, *"Sucks? That's the best an esteemed medical professional can come up with—sucks?"* and, *"it's OK, lie to me. People lie all the time. Go for it. Give it your best lying shot. Be creative in the lying process, make it interesting."* Thus was my official introduction to a bizarre bummer of a medical journey.

My wish list for Christmas, 2009 was the following: the new Shape Ups sneakers to help start me out with my get-fit plan for 2010 (which was strikingly similar to the 2009 get-fit plan I'd abandoned somewhere along February), scented candles to help remove the cigarette smoke smell from my house as soon as I quit, a date with a guy I had a silly teenybopper crush on, a DVD player to watch movies on quiet weekends to replace the one that died just before the warranty I didn't purchase expired, and maybe a Christmas card from my ex-boyfriend Zack, whom I desperately missed and hadn't heard from in a long time.

Here is what I *didn't* wish for: medical bills from an insurance company with a super-high deductible, medications that required tools to dispense and were made from Chinese hamster ovary cells (never having thought of Chinese hamster ovary cells before, I didn't think to specifically not wish for them in a new drug but still …), another reason to prolong my ebbing and flowing depression, a disease.

On that interesting Christmas, which, by the way, is the most beloved holiday of them all for me, I got what I wished for. Well, the sneakers, the candles, and the DVD player anyway. But as is often the case, I also got what I absolutely didn't want. On December 17, I received my diagnosis of multiple sclerosis. MS was not what I was hoping Santa Claus would drop off at my front door. (My little rental house didn't have a fireplace, thus no chimney for the big guy in red.) With the diagnosis came an explanation for at least some of the weirdness going on with me. (Not *all* of it, because, really, can any of us ever explain all the weirdness in our lives?) In some ways, having a name for what was going on in my body did offer some relief just before the holiday.

But in other ways, the timing of the diagnosis was Grinch-like cruel. Who has time to be sick when you are a Christmas maniac like me? I am a total sucker for the season, the music, the decorations, the Nativity and all the hope it promises. And, what my friends didn't understand, the magic of the most wonderful time of the year. It's hard for me not to start humming "God Rest Ye Merry Gentlemen" even thinking about December.

Just one month before that shocking doctor's visit I was trying to describe my love of Christmas to Mya and Dora as we were having dinner. They are two of my dearest friends and, like me, had not been blessed with children of their own. But we all had nieces and nephews. Drew, the oldest and closest of my nephews, was nineteen then, but I still had plenty of little ones to hang up stockings and eat candy canes with. Mya's niece Hannah lived with her and was four at the time: prime Santa Claus age. Mya's family was Laotian and hadn't been brought up with the Christmas mania as I had. I was trying to explain why it was important for Hannah that they take part in all the wonderful festivities.

You see, I was pretty religious and even taught Sunday school at my local church. Although my family was not at all spiritual (I was the reverse black sheep, going to church when the rest of my family refused), we grew up with my mom practically losing her mind about Christmas every year. She loved it and always made it special. We were spoiled on the holiday. But it wasn't the gifts I remembered so fondly, it was the traditions. Guests in and out of our house for two days straight. My mom waking us up with Christmas music after making us sleep in the same room so my oldest sister Laurie would make sure we didn't spy. The tree. The crèche my mom had stained and glazed herself, even though artistic and devout were two of the few things she was not.

I was trying to tell Mya of the magical traditions I had started with Drew when he was younger. How I would take him shopping for a gift for his mom, how we would spend an afternoon making cookies, wrapping gifts, and watching *Prancer* (complete with commercials), which I had taped years before on an old VCR. How I would read him to sleep on Christmas Eve with *How the Grinch Stole Christmas*. I so wanted to share the magic of Christmas with Mya so she could share it with Hannah. The question arose as to what to do when the little ones ask if there really is a Santa Claus, as Dora's seven-year-old nephew had. Jesus is the reason for the season and all the joy and goodwill that comes from it. But for the little ones, Santa Claus is the magic. I told them that they absolutely and in complete sincerity should tell them yes, he is real. Mya is a lawyer and her brain operated in the logistical realm. We began to debate.

She said, "If he is real, then the kids think he is actually coming into their home on Christmas Eve."

"But he *is*," I told her. "Why else would there be presents?"

"But the kids think it is really Santa bringing the presents."

"He is," I argued, "because we all believe he is."

"But he's not really there," insisted Mya, who is usually quite effective at arguing, but was under the influence of what the waiter had described as a "wonderfully crisp and fruity Pinot Grigio" at that point. To try to further prove her point, she introduced me to her invisible friend Tom, sitting across from me. "He's not really here," she said. "But it doesn't matter because I believe that he is."

So I proceeded to introduce myself and get to know Tom.

"Hi, Tom. My name is Yvonne. Have you known Mya long? Are you dating? Can you back me up on this Santa thing? Mya is very stubborn. You're awfully quiet. Are you always this shy when meeting new people?"

My dialogue with him led to a laughing fit that nearly caused me to fall off my chair and Dora to start choking on her wine in between giggles (I guess we all had a little more of the wine than we'd intended). Mya was not amused.

Several weeks later, when Mya, Dora, and another friend, Jenny, came to share with me the magic wonders of the holiday, Tom came too. And I must say, Tom was a lot of fun. The quiet guys can really surprise you sometimes. Kind of like life. Because at that point, everything had changed, and I needed Christmas magic more than ever.

AUGUST IS
A HOT &
STICKY MONTH

In spite of the visit with good friends and getting to spend more time with Mya's imaginary buddy, that December was quite different from any other. The months leading up to the holidays found me struggling with something big, but I didn't know what. The wretchedly hot, humid August after I turned forty was the culmination of what was easy to describe as depression, but I was on antidepressants already and they seemed no match for this misery. I was exhausted all the time. Really exhausted. I was having trouble staying awake on the drive to my job as an office assistant for a doctor and trouble staying awake on the ride home. Not to mention the trouble I was having staying awake while at work and waking up to go back to work after falling asleep on my lunch break. Then one Sunday, I slept all day. Literally, all day. And it was real sleeping too, not the lazy, hanging around, hoping for a breeze, dozing off while casually sipping lemonade sleeping. It was a completely out of it, deep REM sleep for approximately twenty-four hours. And I was not in a medically induced coma. I woke up at noon shocked at the late hour and relieved that religious education classes hadn't started yet, made a cup of tea, and when I woke up again at 6:00 p.m. the tea was still sitting there, never having been touched. Then I ate a bowl of cereal and slept again until my alarm went off Monday morning.

The weekend following my Sleepathon Sunday, my mom and I took a bus trip that consisted of a tour of Block Island. I slept through the boat ride there and back as well as on the bus tour of the island, which embarrassed my mom greatly. But in my defense on that one, Block Island was hot as hell and no one on that island seemed to believe in air conditioning. And every time my mom nudged me awake on the bus tour, the tour operator seemed to be talking about what the island residents did with their waste products. I swear, every time.

Depression seemed to be a likely culprit for my sleepiness. The past year had seen a lot of deaths in my circle including my grandmother (heart attack), my very first love (liver failure), one of my old party buddies (sepsis infection), my friend Killer, who was the husband of my friend Tweety (also heart attack), Dora's boyfriend (cancer), and a mentor who had encouraged my writing (also heart attack). I was also still mourning the breakup with Zack the year before.

Zack was the man I had believed to be my soul mate, and I was still trying to figure out how it could be that you and your soul mate would not be able to make it work. Was it bad timing? Did I misunderstand the meaning of soul mate? Or was it possible (and this is what I was really struggling with) that he really wasn't my soul mate? We were together for two years, happier than I had ever been in a relationship before. And he seemed happy, too.

But then his mother passed away and his father's health declined. Zack felt the need to return to his family in the Midwest and he didn't ask me to go with him. I was still reeling from it. Truly, what would a Cape Cod girl like me do in the landlocked Midwest. A place where fields and farms take the place of water and sand dunes. Where tumbleweeds blow past land meant to lie under seaweed and calves aren't as cute as seals. Where horror stories are told about lonely farmers instead of pirates and everyone talks funny. The Midwest was a crazy world where Starbucks was more popular than Dunkin Donuts and the tolerable smell of dead fish was replaced by the intolerable smell of manure. How would I have survived? Perhaps he was wondering the same thing, and didn't ask me to go with him for that reason. I was devastated just the same. I was willing to take the chance, and he, apparently, was not. How could something that finally felt so right have turned out wrong, and how come we weren't able to figure it out?

Also, I was unhappy at work. I ran the front desk for a medical specialist who excelled in his field, and who was very generous, but who also allowed a lot of drama to transpire in the office. With the extreme fatigue I felt, it was even harder to muster the energy to go to work and deal with who was mad at whom, who might be fired when, and what new problem had been created overnight that I would have to sort out. I had previously been a social worker in a city and could never have dreamed that the petty problems of a small office back home on the Cape would break me down. So many times I felt I was working on a soap opera set. And since TV was another thing that made me sleepy, the soap opera scenario was not helpful. Maybe I should have left the job, but I was trying to obtain the recommended cushion of six months' pay for emergencies before I sought a different career path. And good jobs on Cape Cod were scarce. I was good at the work and I loved interacting with the patients—more reasons to stay put and deal with the drama as best I could.

So there I was that summer, exhausted, smoking a pack of Marlboros every three to four days, and my weight was the highest it had ever been, breaking the 200-pound mark. I knew a lot of it was my fault. I was too tired to exercise and too tired to eat healthy, especially since I hated all vegetables except spinach, which was weird in itself. Every time I would eat spinach to try to be healthy I would think about the E. coli recall of the last year and decide to go to Burger King instead. (Somehow I managed to forget about the salmonella recall of beef two years before and the mad cow disease scare of the last decade. Burger King seemed much safer than E. coli-tainted spinach.)

You would think living near both the ocean and the bay would have offered some relief, at least through the heat. A quick dip in the cool water should wake me up and wipe me of all the icky stickiness the humidity was piling on. Except I had become too tired to even get to the beach! My whole life, the beach had been a refuge. Now it was an exhausting chore. Just the idea of squeezing myself into a bathing suit was overwhelming, never mind walking through thousands of tourists to get to the water. It was far easier to stay home and, well, sleep.

I had mentioned this extreme fatigue to Mandy, my physician's assistant, who recommended blood tests. I had been putting her off, saying I would just get my act together and quit smoking and exercise and eat better and she said I should have done that a long time ago but she wanted the test too. After the Block Island trip I finally agreed. The test showed I had a thyroid condition and would have to take prescription medication. No disrespect to my low-thyroid friends, but all I could think of was that now I would have to list this medication on medical forms like the elderly patients did at my office. The pills helped with the exhaustion, but not completely.

DECK THE MEDICAL HALLS

In November, my mother and I tried another bus trip with some friends. This time it was to Foxwoods Casino in Connecticut to gamble a bit and to see a holiday show. Foxwoods was a trip I had taken regularly with Zack, as he loved it there. He loved it perhaps too much, as we always got cheap or free rooms and almost never paid for dinner. My traveling companions were more interested in the show than the gambling. My mom took thirty dollars to feed into the slot machines and when that was gone, she was done, always. But I loved the excitement of gambling, and I could smoke at the poker table and, as no one else in our group was a smoker, the tables were a perfect hangout. I went from table to table to find one that was hot, leaving only twice to meet my companions for the show and the free buffet that came with the tour ticket, then going back to the tables. I had dressed up a bit and worn black pumps with a slight heel, shoes I wouldn't normally wear to run around in. I had fun and at the end of the day came out $120 richer than when I went in.

The next day my feet tingled, and I figured it was from running around Foxwoods in mini heels. The tingling increased. I felt like I had sand in my shoes, as if the bottoms of my feet were buried in a warm, shallow tidal pool and someone was pouring more sand over the tops of them. To my Cape Codder self, the sensation of sandy feet was almost a comfort. My mom joked that she knew my college boyfriend and I would never make it because when I took him to the beach, he complained to her about the sand in his shoes. (We didn't make it, but I'm not convinced that was the reason.) I didn't think the tingly feeling was a problem since I got it after running around Foxwoods. I took comfort that it came from at least some form of exercise. Then it moved up my legs and the feeling became more like "huh, this seems odd."

My sister Laurie had been diagnosed with MS more than seven years earlier. It had taken doctors over a year to diagnose her. Her main issue was foot drop and balance. She also had terrible migraines and a rare skin condition that increased with heat and stress and would often lead to infection. She struggled greatly. I tried to be supportive of what she was going through, but I am ashamed to admit I mostly took what I knew of the disease solely from what she told me. On my own, I never really looked into it. I didn't read up on it or completely understand what the shots she had to take were for. I kept meaning to and for years had on my list of things to do a list of websites I should check out to learn more about her challenges. I never did. Instead I bought books for her to read and called regularly and listened when she needed to talk. What I understood about her actual diagnosis was pretty much nothing at all, as I later learned.

So it wasn't surprising that I didn't think of MS when I woke up ten days after the Foxwoods trip and the tingling had progressed to numbness and reached past my knees. It was hard to tell when and where my legs were numb as opposed to when and where they were tingly. They were pretty much just a strange, sensational mess. Since I was not sure I would be able to stand when I got out of bed, my thought was that perhaps I should try to figure this out. I called my doctor's office and they suggested I come in. I told Laurie and she gave me what amounted to field sobriety tests to do at home to find out if it was MS. I passed two out of three. I was able to touch the tip of my nose without missing and stand on one leg, purposely hopping on the leg to give myself extra credit. But I couldn't walk the line without falling off. Since I didn't have an actual line in my house, I didn't consider that a complete failure. But since I had studied and practiced for these tests a lot in my younger years, falling off the imaginary line was still a slight concern.

"It is not MS," Laurie said. "It just couldn't be." As I had never looked into the specifics of MS, I gladly agreed with her.

One month before the problem with my legs, I had had a standard mammogram because, as my primary care doc, Dr. N, told me, I have 'lumpy boobs'. I didn't really know what 'lumpy boobs' were from a diagnostic perspective, but I took her word for it. This was at the same time that new recommendations came out stating women should have mammograms less often. However, I was not only willing to have a mammogram, I was almost eager because I had recently obtained Aflac short-term disability insurance and they would pay me seventy-five dollars to have a cancer screening annually. What would one do for seventy-five dollars? For me, the answer was: get my boobs mashed. (The next year I underwent a Pap smear Mandy said could wait a year just so I could get the check. She told me of all the reasons she had heard to get a Pap smear that was the first.) The mammography technologist found a spot on the mammogram and needed to do it again.

So on the Friday before Thanksgiving, I worked until noon so I could get to my mammogram appointment at 1:00. I was due to see Mandy at 3:00, but I figured I could make it with time to spare. I was pretty convinced that the spot was nothing (probably just one of the normal lumps in my aforementioned lumpy boobs) and was more worried about the leg thing, but I got my boobs mashed again anyway. To help pass the time, I pictured the Aflac duck swooping around the mammogram machine, his flapping wings causing my bra to wave about the room.

The technologist next told me I needed an ultrasound to further examine the mysterious spot. Now I was starting to get nervous and told them no matter what, I had to be out of there by 2:30. They put the goop on me and moved a wand around my breast. Next, a male doctor came in and introduced himself to me and my exposed boob. Then, without even buying me dinner first, he proceeded to feel me up. As he rubbed and pressed my mammary area, getting his hands covered in the ultrasound goop, he chatted about his wife. Turns out she was a colleague of my boss, so he must have thought talking about her would be good boob-stroking conversation. Once he was done, he wiped his hand with a tissue and told me that the spot was fine and nothing to worry about. Then he told me that I shouldn't listen to the media and should come back every year to do this again. I nodded, point made. Then I made my own point to him, although I didn't mean to. As I sat up and slid my numb legs off the table the left one bumped the doctor's crotch none too lightly. I tried to apologize but he waved me off and exited the room quickly, a little hunched over. I didn't do it on purpose, and with the numbness, my legs didn't have much motion so I don't think the pain was too great. But if they were putting me through this humiliating process of boob-mashing just to make a point about the need for yearly mammograms, then I guess I got them back. And the co-pays for all of that probably came to about $500 so it was a good thing I got seventy-five dollars from Aflac.

Next I went to Mandy, who focused on my legs. She poked and tickled and pounded and then told me to hold on while she got a fork. Wait, a FORK???? What was she going to do with a fork? Were we taking a break for lunch? Was she going to force-feed me veggies to make sure I wasn't lying about improving my diet? But the fork she was talking about was supersized, likely made for the Jolly Green Giant as he feasted on corn niblets. It was metal and looked sterile and I had a few tense seconds to wonder what she planned to do with that thing. She used it to poke and tap and prod some more and then agreed something was going on and we needed to do some tests. She told me not to worry about it too much until we had more information. Thing was, now that she had done all her stuff and agreed something was up, I was less worried and more relieved that I wasn't going crazy.

Three weeks later I was off to see a new specialist, Dr. Zemanek, to be electrocuted. He was a handsome Czechoslovakian doctor with a cool accent who had me take off my slacks, put a paper towel around my butt, and lie down. Good thing I had thought to wear decent underwear. He then proceeded to electrocute various parts of my legs. At least, that is what it seemed like he was doing. The actual test was called an Electromyogram and involved sticking electrodes all over your legs and then measuring the electrical activity from your nerves to your muscles. I didn't even know that I HAD electrical activity going from my nerves to my muscles. If I have electricity in me then why are my utility bills so damn high?

I had been worried about pain because when I looked up FAQs on the EMG online, the first question was, "Does the test hurt?" and the answer was a blatant, "Yes, the test hurts."

It didn't hurt really, but didn't feel too great either, and lying there being zapped (even by a handsome Czech doctor) was a little unnerving. It sounded like an electric bug swatter as it zzzzed, zzzed, zzzed … Whatever it was supposed to show, it didn't, so

I thought *cool, there is nothing up.* But Dr. Zemanek said no. While I might enjoy the sensation of sand in my toes, I should only be walking on the beach when I got it. I tried to distract him and my own worried thoughts by recommending that he take a few walks on the beach to see what it was like. "It really is beautiful and the sand between your toes is like a natural foot scrub." He didn't seem interested and said my primary care provider would call me. And ten minutes later, as I was walking into the mall to Christmas shop while I could still walk, Mandy did call. It was time for MRIs.

CRYING FOR CHARITY IN KMART

As if weird leg issues weren't enough of a concern, the holidays were adding other stresses. In addition to making me crazy, the stresses just added more exhaustion to my already exhausted self. Church, normally a place of peace and refuge, was one example. I had taught Sunday school for three years and then stopped when I was living with Zack. It didn't seem right to be spouting wholesome Christian values while I was "living in sin." After Zack left, I discovered my church was in need of teachers and volunteered to teach again.

I loved my seventh grade Sunday school class, a small group of six kids, but had managed to put us in the middle of a mini-religious education Christmas pageant scandal. It began at our religious education staff meeting, when the pageant director announced she had a migraine and was having trouble concentrating. Under this inauspicious beginning, we started preparations for the holiday event. The director stated that since the older kids wouldn't want to dress up as angels and sheep, they could be in charge of pageant tech work by setting up chairs, decorating, and serving refreshments. My seventh graders were the oldest of the group. I told them the plan and they were ecstatic. But as the performance got closer, the director didn't seem to recall her original directive. In fact, she was shocked at the idea that my class wouldn't be on stage singing.

"But we never talked about them singing," I tried to explain. "I thought we said it was only the younger kids performing."

"I don't remember a decision where one of the classes wouldn't be on stage and wouldn't be participating!" she insisted.

To complicate matters (or perhaps explain the sudden importance of singing for my class), the smaller children in the pageant weren't really doing that great with the performing aspect. Rehearsals were filled with chaos and the glad caroling was more like a whisper of tiny voices in the vast, acoustically challenging church hall.

Soon one or two other teachers began to think of my class as a bunch of uncooperative, difficult preteens who were intent on ruining Christmas for the whole parish by not being willing to sing. It seemed that I had unwittingly turned them into a group of semi-delinquents. Perhaps I took other people's stress too personally, but I couldn't help feeling like my class had been set up. We had our plan laid out and now plans were changed, but we hadn't been allowed to catch up. In the end I apologized to the kids for the confusion and they were troupers. They sang their hearts out, towering high above first-grade sheep who spent the pageant shearing themselves by plucking off their cotton ball wool, second-grade angels whispering rather than shouting the news of the birth of Christ, and an assortment of other kids tugging at their costumes, eager to get to the punch and cookies. I cringed with my group during the silly-kids rendition of "We Wish You a Merry Christmas" and tried to make the pageant mess up to them with fun classes in the New Year.

Then there was family drama. My nephew Drew called to tell me that his mom and grandmother had gotten into a nasty argument. Some very upsetting things were said. Drew worried that his mom would not join us for Christmas. I was tired, grouchy, and stressed, and all I could think to say to my nephew was, "Listen Drew, Christmas is my holiday and it is very important to me. I will have the decorations lit, music playing, and a nice dinner cooking. Everyone is welcome, but this holiday is about peace, love, and joy and anyone who is not about peace, love, and joy can get the fuck out!"

"Fair enough, Auntie, fair enough."

Perhaps swearing during the holiday is not very Christian-like but the Bible doesn't say not to and who knows if Mary didn't utter a curse or two during that manger delivery.

Next up in the stress of 'everyday things that shouldn't be so freaking stressful, but they are' department, was preparing for the holiday at work. In the past, we had done a Christmas party with a Secret Santa gift swap and gone in together on a present for our boss, Dr. T. This year, he had told us not to get him any gifts as "there is nothing you could possibly get me that I would want, need, or use." But we wanted to do something special for him as he was always very generous to his staff, especially during the holidays. We had also previously signed up with an organization that offered folks a chance to buy presents for a child whose family was struggling financially and wouldn't be able to buy their own presents. A company would "adopt" the child and then fill his or her Christmas wish list. The organization would deliver your gifts to the parents of the child, who would wrap and present them as coming from Santa Claus.

We decided that since we had some new staff members whom we didn't know very well, it made more sense to adopt two kids this season and skip giving each other and Dr. T a gift. Jackie became the office employee in charge of this project. She wasn't in charge of much and this wasn't rocket science. She loved being in charge of this, however, as the agency communicated with her directly and had the idea that she was "Mrs. Dr. T," which she thought was a riot. Jackie notified the agency of our intention and they sent us the names and wish lists of two kids, a boy and a girl. Problem was, the boy they matched us with really wanted a bicycle, a big-ticket item, and one we weren't sure we could really afford. I asked Jackie if she thought we could handle that request and, if not, we should trade him for another child so that his wish might be fulfilled.

"Well, we can get him other things," she stated.

"No, we really can't," I said. "It is his Christmas wish list and he really should get the bike. If we can't do it, maybe someone else can."

It became a big back and forth issue with everyone coming to me to discuss it. Jackie, meanwhile, spent a lot of time online looking at bikes instead of working but never took a step towards actually purchasing one. Somehow the discussion made its way to Dr. T, and he said he would get the bike. Then he changed his mind and said he would just give the boy his daughter's old bike.

"You can't do that, Dr. T. That is not fair to him. The idea behind the program is that these kids get nice, new gifts," I told him.

This is how things went at my office. Fellow employees liked to discuss things, disagree, think about them, research them online, and plan, but in the end, it was usually me who had to sort out whatever it was and explain the solution to the boss. More issues came up, and with each issue, the fatigue amplified.

It was too late by that time to give this little boy's list to another group who could fulfill his bike wishes. In the end, Dr. T came through. He asked his wife to purchase a bicycle and then he spent the morning telling me about the big argument it caused with her claiming she didn't have time, him claiming she did, and the argument that escalated from there. We all got other things for the little girl and some clothes and small toys for the boy, except for Terry who was in the middle of finals at her night school. She was willing to participate but didn't have the time. Jackie, who had already done her shopping, agreed to do it for her. But she waited until the last minute. When Dr. T announced she needed to work on an afternoon she was supposed to have off, she told him she would be happy to work and then when he was gone, proceeded to complain to me about it and state now that she had to work, she wouldn't be able to shop for Terry. Terry was off and in major study mode. The gifts had to be turned in the next day.

And that is how I found myself, at noon that same day, doing Terry's shopping that Jackie was supposed to do for the little boy Dr. T. had bought a bike for. There was torrential, cold rain outside and I was on my lunch break, parked way out in left field due to the holiday crowds and limping with my numb, tingling legs into Kmart. I hate Kmart. Please don't think I am a shopping snob. I love discounts, I cut coupons, and I get most of my clothes from the closeout rack whenever possible. But in the words of Dustin Hoffman in *Rainman*, "Kmart sucks!" It is always too hot in the summer and too cold in the winter. There are always two cashiers when they need six and no one to help you on the floor, ever. And half the things aren't priced and if they are, they are priced wrong. But it was forty-five minutes closer to work than Walmart (my usual choice) and I had a one hour lunch break and about thirty dollars of Terry's money to spend, so Kmart it was.

I went through that store like a maniac. I'm sure I looked like a drunk with my poor walking skills. Who knows if it was the tingling in my feet or the numbness in my legs that caused the shuffling gait, but shuffling was how I was moving. With each step, there was a slight worry that a leg or two might give out, but I tried to ignore the worry. Despite this, I found what I thought were good deals on both toys and games in record time, items that could be given to both kids. Then I stepped into the outrageously long checkout line as I watched the time ticking off on my break. I was hungry (this was supposed to be my lunch break, after all) but I had no expectations of actually getting lunch. Grabbing a bag of M&Ms from the candy aisle to munch on the ride back was the best I could hope for. Finally, the line wound down to just one woman in front of me, who proceeded to argue about the price of everything in her cart.

"Why is this roll of toilet paper ringing up at 99 cents when the sign said it was 96 cents?" She was probably right and tried to draw me into her argument with the cashier but I was tired, wet, cold, hungry, hurting, and mad. Jackie/"Mrs. Doctor," who had said she would do this and only worked part-time even with added hours, should have been the one stuck here in Kmart trying to make two kids' Christmas dreams come true. I could care less about the price of toilet paper.

A manager was called over. The line grew, as did my exhaustion. People in back of us grumbled. My legs ached. The woman in front argued some more. And to my shock, I started to cry. It was all just too much. I wanted to give up and go home. But it was Christmas and this was for deserving children, so I forced myself to stop crying in order to get it done. When my turn came and the cashier rang up my items, I discovered that things from the sale table weren't really on sale and the items that were "two for one" meant only if you bought two of the same color. Now I was in exactly the same position as the arguing woman, but I didn't have the energy to protest or start all over again. I also didn't have the time. I supplemented the thirty dollars from Terry with sixty dollars of my own money on top of the fifty dollars I had already put in for my own gifts, hoping at least that the kids would like their presents.

I had pulled myself together during the checkout but carrying the bags to the car in the downpour undid me once again. Through tears of frustration and exhaustion, and the rain beating on my windshield, I called Jackie to tell her I would be late returning from my break because of the chaos in Kmart. She responded with a bit of attitude as it was now five minutes past the time for her break to start. When I got back, achy and soaked and emotionally drained, I put the bags down. Jackie reached out to go through them and I grabbed them out of her hands so fast she didn't know what happened.

No way was she going to ignore the phone while gushing over presents I just went through a nightmare and way too much money to buy. Only the reminder that Christmas was about love, not violence, kept me from smacking her over the head with one of those not-such-a-great deal-after-all hard plastic toys. She must have seen the menace in my eyes, and she wisely backed off.

I grabbed the gifts away from her and neither of us said a word. When she came in the following week and asked me if the gifts got to the agency okay and I told her they had, she remarked how it made her feel so good to go out and do something for someone else. Yeah, warm fuzzies all over. Again, I felt like punching her but held back, reminding myself that it was still the season of peace, love, and joy. And also that Mya, my friend and promised lawyer "on retainer for life," was in the middle of a big trial. If I gave in to my base impulse, it would take her forever to get away and bail me out.

Helping others during the season of love wasn't done wreaking havoc with me. Remember how I said I was a Christmas maniac? Well, that extended to every aspect of my life. I was a member of the Lion's Club, and months before I had signed up to help with a town-wide Holiday Festival. But after several inquiries I never heard any more about it. I was relieved as I was just so very tired and overwhelmed. Two days before the event however, the woman in charge finally returned my call.

"So we'll see you Saturday. We'll need you there by eight. The event lasts until two but with clean up, volunteers are usually out by three, four at the latest."

"What? How come you didn't respond sooner?" I asked. "When I didn't hear from you I thought you must have had everyone you needed. This is the first I have heard about it since November."

"Oh, well I only just found out the details," she claimed.

Spending a Saturday working at a holiday fair was the last thing I needed. What I needed was to crawl into bed and rest. I needed to try to sleep away the aches that now included not just my legs but my head and torso too. I needed to rest or do something to beat this bug or whatever it was that had taken me over. But I had said I would do it and I was going to have a joyful Christmas, dammit, and so I went. The frustration increased when the woman who recruited me showed up two hours late. But here was the silver lining in the Christmas fair cloud. By arriving at 8:00 a.m., I managed to stake my preferred volunteer claim.

I was assigned to the table helping kids make magic Christmas dust, which, of course, is a very important part of the holiday. So even though everything in my body was hurting, the noise and commotion of hundreds of excited kids were making my head want to explode, and being on my feet for seven hours on a Saturday made me even more wobbly than usual, I loved making that magic Christmas dust.

I made some magic dust for Hannah and told Mya very clearly that you put it on your lawn on Christmas Eve so that if it is cloudy, the glitter will light the way for Santa and the reindeer will smell the oats and Santa Claus will still find you. She omitted a key part of my basic instructions. She and Hannah had ceremoniously put the dust out two weeks before Christmas and waited anxiously for the magic to happen. After five days of nothing happening except a whole lot of small animals suddenly becoming interested in Mya's parents' lawn, Mya called me to complain that her parents were wondering what the hell was on their lawn that was attracting tons of birds and bird poop and Hannah was wondering why Santa hadn't shown up yet.

◆ ◆ ◆ ◆

This was the brilliant time I decided to quit smoking. Likely not the best time with all that was going on but the timing of the decision wasn't completely my choice. I had been an off and on smoker for many of my adult years, but with the heartbreak of Zack leaving, I became more of a regular one. Cigarettes were my friends. They were my bad-for-you, take-you-down-the-wrong-path-and-then-leave-you-stranded friends, but my friends nonetheless. They comforted me when I felt miserable. Or, at least, they made me think they were comforting me. They convinced me that it was okay to give in to my weary and sad thoughts while I puffed away on them.

Anna was my friend too, but a real one. She was a very kind, hard-working, good friend. We had met at work and managed to stay friends and grow close through most of the office pettiness and politics. She was going through a difficult pregnancy but was holding her own until baby Emma decided she wanted out two and a half months early. Anna was in and out of the hospital and on complete bed rest to avoid going into labor, and the situation was serious.

I was worrying about Anna and her baby as I smoked one of my cigarette friends, and the idea came to me to make a bargain with God. Now, usually I don't believe in bargaining with God. Frankly, I think he just laughs at you when you do. Do people actually think he's weighing these requests seriously? *Dear God, I will never, ever say your name in vain again if you help me win a million dollars. Dear God, if you please, please, please help me get tickets to the next Rolling Stones concert, I swear, I will never ask for anything again.* But I so wanted Anna and her husband to have a healthy child that I was willing to try anything. I put out that cigarette and crushed the other five in my pack, and I told God that if he would just make little Emma healthy I would never smoke again.

That was December 9. Little Emma was born beautiful and healthy on January 27. I was so happy for her parents and she was just the most precious thing. What a relief! And I was smoke free. Perhaps I was breathing better but I was still exhausted and whiny and no longer had my cigarette friends to whine to. I considered going back on my "deal," now that the baby was here and healthy. Then it occurred to me that I had specifically said "little" Emma when I was making that deal. What is little? There was no end date on my bargain. In some views, she could be little forever. Now God was laughing at what a dummy his servant was, whether or not he was in on the bargain. Maybe when Emma is thirty years old, if she is over six feet and the champion of the Women's Professional Wrestling team, striking terror in the heart and soul of her opponents, I would be able to smoke? I will be seventy then, and hopefully I won't want to.

PROCLAIMING THE SUCKY NEWS

The weird sensations continued and changed. It now felt like my underwear was falling down. I would find myself at work constantly trying to yank up the waistband on my underwear, only to find it was right where it was supposed to be, and then wondering if anyone had caught me tugging at my pants. Mandy said I wasn't crazy and that gave me hope. It was the start of the last full work week before Christmas, and I managed to fit in four MRIs. The first two of the spine were a cakewalk. I knew people said you could get claustrophobic but as far as I knew, I didn't have a tendency toward that and I was pleased that the MRI process wasn't as bad as I expected. The next day was completely different.

Have you ever had a brain MRI? Have you ever had it done with injected dye for contrast and a brand new technician who is not very friendly and more importantly, not able to find a vein? Picture the technician disappearing while running the test instead of doing the usual reassuring check-ins, like "Halfway through the cycle now!" and "Almost done! You're doing great!" Throughout the ten-hour MRI, I kept thinking of the Stephen King novel where a girl is handcuffed to a bed and trapped for days until she eventually has to chew off her own thumb to get out. Trapped in this tube with my head clamped into a viselike grip that I was not getting out of even if the world ended while I was in there, since I wouldn't be able to chew off my own head if it was necessary, I was screwed. I'm sure the test wasn't really ten hours, but with the tech disappearing for long periods of time doing who knows what, it really felt like it.

I stumbled out of the hospital, dazed and scared for the first time since this all began. This test had been serious and intense. The doctors must be looking for something serious and intense. What was wrong with me and how bad would it be? Before the brain MRI, I just thought my body was acting weird. Now I began to panic. Would this never go away? And if not, would it get worse? How much worse could it get? Would I stop being able to walk?

I called the hospital the next morning to find out what would happen from here. Before having the MRIs, I hadn't even bothered to ask what the next step would be. But the tingling in my legs and abdomen was getting stronger, sometimes feeling like I was being lightly pricked all over my lower body with pins. As the sensation was traveling up my body, soon it would reach my chest, neck, and head. I had already been suffering regular headaches and didn't think I could take any more spasms attacking my overtaxed brain. Suddenly I wanted answers. Now! Luckily, I didn't have to wait long. Two hours later my primary care physician called me at work and after making sure I could talk (I really couldn't as the office was busy but my need to know overwhelmed me), she gently told me that I had multiple sclerosis. She said I needed to get to a Boston hospital immediately and should be prepared to stay. Stunned, I blurted the news to my coworkers. I told them I needed to leave right away, that I wouldn't be back that day and no, I didn't know when I'd be back. Then I left, mumbling "I don't know" to all their other questions, desperate to get outside and away from spectators. In the car I realized I had made that announcement in front of several patients, which was unprofessional and not like me at all.

Surprisingly, I didn't cry. Two thoughts were going through my mind:

1. How am I going to do this since I am completely terrified of driving in Boston?

2. I can't stay in the hospital now, Christmas is next week!

First, to deal with the drive. I tried to reach Drew to see if he could drive me but he wasn't home. He was living with my mom at that time, which meant that when I called, I had to tell her what was going on as minimally as I could and insist she NOT come, as she was no better driving in the city than I was and having a passenger would just stress me out more. Laurie was in New Hampshire and was a worse city driver than both of us put together. I called Mya, who lived and worked forty-five minutes outside of the city and, as she worked for herself, would be able to leave and meet me at the hospital. She said she would call me once she got there to try to find a place to connect or at least to help guide me over the phone.

I was proceeding up the Cape's main highway but I don't remember much. At some point I decided to make another call, my apologies to Oprah for driving and talking. This time I called Christopher, my twenty-one-year-old half-brother. My dad and stepmother had been in Aruba for two weeks and Chris and I had chatted while they were gone. I had invited him over for dinner just the week before but as I am not renowned for my cooking, and I told him that dinner was boxed pasta and jarred sauce, he didn't make it. But I had mentioned the sensation weirdness to him and to my half-sister Suzanne, who lived out of state. I didn't want to call him. He was attending a nearby college. It was finals week and I had no idea where he was with them. Was he done with finals? Did he have more studying to do? And I didn't want to be the weak one. I was much older than him. I don't like being the one to ask for help. But I did call, got his voice mail and hung up. He called back only seconds later to ask what was up.

Me: "Where are you?"

Him: "At a buddy's house."

Me: "Are you taking a final?"

Him: "No, I am at a buddy's house."

Me: "Do you have any finals today?"

Him: "No, what is going on?"

Me: "Nothing, what is going on with you? What are you doing today?"

Him: "WHAT IS GOING ON???????"

"Ok, here's the deal. That weird thing that has been going on, my doc called and told me I had to get to a hospital in Boston and I may have to stay and I am terrified of driving in Boston and don't want to leave my car there so I was going to see if you would take me but only if you are done with finals and really not doing anything otherwise I will just drive myself and Mya can meet me there and I will figure it out."

"Where are you now?"

"Almost at the Bridge."

"Can I drive your car?"

"Better than I can, I'm sure." Christopher was a dirt bike, speed boat, anything-that-is-fast maritime student who had been driving trucks since he was nine and boats probably long before that.

"Meet me at my school in fifteen minutes."

And there he was, standing at the bed of his huge pickup, tying down his two dirt bikes in the back of the truck.

"Now I see why you want to take my car. Will those be okay here?"

"Yes, people know they are mine and won't touch them."

Chris has a healthy dose of my father's "nobody's going to mess with me on my turf" attitude and so far, it has served them both well.

The speed demon got us to the hospital in record time. The first comforting thing I discovered was that it was easy to get to this hospital as it was right off the highway, and I knew I could get there by myself if I had too. The second thing was the statues of the Virgin Mary outside and in the lobby and the symbols of St. Elizabeth. With Christmas on my mind, I assumed the St. Elizabeth the hospital was named for was the mother of John the Baptist whom I have always been especially endeared to. The woman received her own miracle, and was more than happy to love and raise the martyr who would herald and die for the coming Messiah. I have always been fond of those who treasure playing second fiddle. The third and best comforting thing was that Mya was standing in the lobby and had become familiar with the place already.

"This is the floor we have to get to," she said. "This elevator."

"Are you sure?" I asked. "There are several elevators—A, B, C …"

Her look clearly said, "Are you seriously doubting me now?" and we followed her to the place we needed to be. It was comforting to have them both with me. Chris is a handsome kid, popular with those of the female persuasion and likened himself to my charming, flirtatious dad. Mya is attractive, stylish, and witty but in a no-nonsense kind of way. With Chris' charm and Mya's wit, they quickly fell into a kind of funny sibling relationship, taking me with them. Mya acted as my older, wiser sister, even though she was a few years younger than me. Chris took on the part of the protective older brother, even though he was many, many years younger than me. I was by far the oldest of our group but you wouldn't have known it the way they took over and guided me through the hospital, Mya in the lead, Chris backing her up and looking out for us both, and me simply lost in the new location and the unexpected set of circumstances.

Chris had always been fond of Mya ever since I brought her and my friends Julie and Samantha to his house years before, and my dad took all of us out to the beach over the four-wheel-drive trails. Chris was nine and already playing host to the attractive "older women." Making sure everyone was comfortable he told us, "Here is some wine and a towel. Hold on, because the ride gets a little bumpy. And if you get hot, just push this button to roll down the window."

When Mya saw how beautiful the beach was, she became annoyed with me that I hadn't told her to bring a bathing suit (it was Cape Cod in the summer after all) and proceeded to jump into the Atlantic fully and fashionably dressed. Chris never forgot how cool that was. Later that day, when Samantha realized she forgot her pocketbook in the back of my dad's truck, we drove back to the house to get it. We saw the truck turning around on the busy road in front of their driveway, and my dad emptying the cooler in the yard. I freaked when I realized it was Chris driving.

"But Yvonne, he's an excellent driver," Julie rationalized.

"He's nine!" I argued.

That was Chris, confidently in control even at a young age. He thought Mya was cool and he knew he was cool. Thus it was that I had two calm, cool allies walking the very uncool, very flustered, wobbly me through the hospital.

When I was filling out paperwork I made the brilliant move of telling the front desk that I brought my lawyer with me to check out everything. It was a nervous joke, but in her courtroom suit, Mya certainly looked the part.

"Nice, Yvonne, smart move," Chris said, and I realized why nervousness leads to idiocy. Was it my imagination or did the staff look at Mya suspiciously all day? Mya went into the doctor's office with me and we left Chris in the lobby with nothing to do and nowhere to go, as there wasn't much to do around this part of the city. But there was a Bible in the waiting room and I had been his Confirmation sponsor. It was my role to always guide him in the ways of Christianity, goodness, and light in the world.

"Here," I said, giving it to him. "Start with Luke and you'll get the whole Christmas story including the story of the patron saint of the hospital." (Later I learned that St. Elizabeth's is actually named for Elizabeth of Hungary, who is still a cool second fiddle type in her own right.) When I came out to check on him later and introduce him to my new doctor, he was sound asleep. So much for guidance.

Mya was there when the male physician's assistant did more poking, prodding, stabbing, and questioning.

"Do you feel this?"

"Yes."

"And when I tap your leg here, do you feel that?"

"No."

"How about here?"

"Yes."

"And here?"

"No."

"I think you are just alternating between 'yes' and 'no' to my questions," he said.

"Probably," I admitted. I didn't mean to be a difficult patient but at this point I wasn't sure what I felt where anymore.

He asked me more general questions and Mya refrained from comment when I admitted I had been smoking regularly for a while but that I had quit for good two weeks before.

After my initial exam with her assistant, Dr. M came in, introduced herself, and verified that I had MS by showing me my MRI with what looked like a huge brain tumor in it, practically the size of my whole head.

"No," Dr. M calmly stated. "It is not a brain tumor, it is an MS lesion."

"Are you sure it is not a brain tumor?" I asked. "Because it really, really looks like a brain tumor."

She went on to explain that MS lesions are different from brain tumors as one of them has scalloped edges, and that is how you tell. Scalloped edges? What do scallops have to do with this? What did they do? Scallops are my favorite seafood, and my mind whirled thinking this illness had something to do with seafood. I was very confused. As far as the medical people know, scallops do not have anything to do with MS. But you can see how my brain was handling the news.

I asked Dr. M if MS was the reason I had been a klutz all my life.

"No, absolutely not," was her response.

My question and Dr. M's answer would be repeated by Mya to all of our friends with great amusement many times in the future.

Dr. M explained that I had the relapsing-remitting form of multiple sclerosis and I knew from Laurie, as she had it too, that it was the least dangerous form of the disease. Still, Dr. M said, "I'm not going to lie to you—MS sucks. You and I are going to become good friends." I guessed that meant I would be visiting Dr. M a lot. I'd better get used to the place.

She hugged me then and introduced me to the nurses who explained how I would have to give myself shots (WHATTTTT?) and did I want a surface shot three days a week or a muscle shot once a week. How about no shots? That was what I wanted, no shots. That option sounded good.

But that was not an option. I picked the surface subcue (later I learned that the word was subcutaneous and meant "just under the skin") something or other shots as that's what my sister did, and then they sent me to see a nice woman named Sally where I kept failing this game where you had to use one hand to put pegs in a board. It wasn't that I couldn't put the pegs in the board, but that I kept forgetting to use only one hand and would use both and then we would have to start over. We had to do the peg board game test about four times before I remembered to use only one hand. I didn't know what they were testing but if it was the brain to see if I could remember instructions, then I definitely failed. Then Sally had me walk really fast down the hall for thirty seconds. I aced that test. I had grown up working in the tourist industry in Provincetown and in my teen years was too poor to waste money on a tourist-priced hot dog. I had only twenty minutes to get home and back for lunch while dodging baby strollers, sexy male Cher impersonators on scooters, men in Speedos holding hands, families gawking at men wearing Speedos holding hands, fish trucks, and rent-a-cops on the main street. Compared to that, thirty seconds in an empty hallway was a breeze—even stumbling and off-kilter, I still had that one down.

Next, my MS support posse and I were sent to a different area of the hospital, where I was shot up with steroids for one hour. I teased Chris about the gorgeous female hematologist, while he and Mya did a Sudoko together. He told Mya how the needle they were plunging into me was nothing compared to the needle he had to have when he broke his ankle after last year's dirt bike accident. The accident where he swore he wasn't doing any jumps as opposed to the seven or eight bones he had broken previously when he was doing stunts.

I was relieved that I didn't have to stay overnight. We left the hospital and met Julie for dinner (which was the fourth comforting thing of the traumatic day) and Chris tried to cheer me up by telling me I could get a handicapped parking plate. They all agreed this was a good idea. I wasn't so sure I was ready for that.

Chris was vehement. "Even if you don't want to use it right now, you could give it to me."

"Christopher, you are twenty-one years old, you drive a huge Ford F150 with two dirt bikes in the back, and you're going to park in a handicapped spot?"

"Sure, why not?"

We managed to laugh at this and it felt good to be laughing with my little brother and my friends.

On the drive back to the Cape, Chris and I chatted and bonded the whole time like we had never chatted and bonded before, and that was the fifth comforting thing that had happened that day. I asked Chris if he had gotten me a Christmas present yet, knowing full well that our sister Suzanne bought all the Christmas presents for them both and would then hit him up for cash afterwards. I handed him the incredibly huge green binder about the drug I had to take and told him to take it home, put a bow on it and then give it back to me next week and he would be all set. He didn't. When I looked through the binder later I was miffed that it was missing the free pen and magnifying glass it promised on the first page.

"Do you really need a magnifying glass?" Mya demanded.

"No, but I'll take all the freebies I can get right now." I had been diagnosed with relapsing-remitting multiple sclerosis. The least the universe could do was give me a free pen and magnifying glass.

I also called my boss on the way home and he said all the kind, appropriate things bosses say: "I'm so sorry to hear that. I'm so sorry you're going through this. Whatever I can do to help. Take all the time you need. Let me know if there is anything I can do," etc., etc.

Once I got home, I grabbed the mail on my way into the house. It was eight days before Christmas, but I didn't have any Christmas cards or holiday bills. The only piece of mail in my mailbox that day was a solicitation ... from the National MS Society.

Oh, the irony.

I used the postage-paid envelope they included to ask them to make me a member.

A HOLY WEEK, OR THE FUZZY BATHROBE

All I needed from my boss right away was the next day off for my first infusion at the local hospital. In the aftermath of the medical news, avoidance reigned supreme. Maybe I was still in shock, or maybe it was the fact that Christmas was the following week, but I didn't think about MS. Mostly, I was just excited about not having to go to work that Friday. Instead of taking the time to process all that had happened and all that I had been told, I figured I now had some much-needed time to catch up on my holiday to-do list. First, I slept late. Then, as I began to pull my day together, I decided to go to the post office for stamps for the cards I could definitely get out now that I didn't have to spend the weekend in the hospital. This morning of errands began with a series of mix-ups.

At the post office I saw that our Lions donations box was chock full of eyeglasses that needed to be emptied. I was our club's official eyeglass gatherer, cleaner, and packer. I was embarrassed that I hadn't known we had a box here and was unprepared to take the glasses. I asked the Postmaster if he happened to have a shopping bag lying around I could use. He seemed annoyed, but said, "I guess I could give you this one to take. But where's Bernie?" *Who the hell is Bernie,* I thought. *We are only women in our group and I don't know any Bernie.*

"Excuse me, who's Bernie?"

"Uh, the guy from the Lions who collects the eyeglasses," he replied with skepticism in his tone.

I started emptying the box figuring the Postmaster was out of his mind. He kept eyeing me as he tended to other customers. I was almost finished when the box shifted a bit and I saw the words:

"If box is full, please call Bernie at 508-XXX-XXXX" with another club's name clearly written underneath.

I was pilfering another club's eyeglass collection! At Christmas, no less. It never occurred to me that another club might cover the same area. I began to put the glasses back, which seemed to make the Postmaster even more suspicious. I tried to explain, but he was busy and no longer interested in what explanations I was mumbling. I bet he called Bernie as soon as it quieted down though. I could just imagine the phone conversation: "Hey Bernie, there's this girl going around pretending to be a Lion and she tried taking your glasses. I scared her out of the post office for you. Don't worry, they're all here."

Next was what should have been a simple ATM withdrawal from the bank. Except when I left the parking lot after finishing at the ATM, I realized I hadn't taken my card out of the machine. I circled back quickly and was relieved to see that no one else had gotten to the ATM. My card had popped out and was just patiently waiting for me. Until I went to grab it and the machine chose that second to suck it back up. I frantically pushed button after button, but the machine insisted on keeping my card. With the window rolled down, and in a panic, I sped around the building. A man with a little girl approximately five or so yelled, "What's the matter with you? Slow down!"

He was right. I was driving way too fast in the parking lot. I called out to him.

"Sir, I'm awfully sorry. The machine ate my card and I am a little panicked but I shouldn't have been driving so fast."

"I was talking to my daughter," the man said. "She likes to run down the ramp and I've told her a thousand times not to do that."

"Oh, I'm sorry, I thought you meant me and you would be right. I was driving way too fast."

"I was talking to my kid." He was annoyed now and my apology was getting nowhere.

I parked, waited in the long line and then explained my plight to a teller. She informed me that I had to come back later in the day for the card. Apparently the machine liked to slowly savor cards a bit before they regurgitated them back to their spacey owners. I was really late for the infusion now, so I headed up the highway.

My whole life I had been taught not to speed in this section of the Cape, the town of Eastham. Even my dad, the cool Provincetown cop, warned against it. "Those cops in Eastham don't fool around. Whatever you do, don't speed in Eastham."

I had warned my friends who came down to visit me as well. You weren't a native of Cape Cod if you didn't appreciate that golden rule. But I was late for my second infusion, the first at my local hospital.

I had also always been told that is was okay to drive ten miles or so over the speed limit. There was a patrol car in the passing lane, doing about forty-five, five miles over the limit on that stretch of highway. Not ten, but five, so I figured I still had room. I approached in the right lane. I passed him. Forty-seven, fifty, fifty-two, fifty-four, fifty-six, fifty-nine, and then the lights. He was behind me now, but he couldn't possibly mean me. I was only going just a bit over the limit. But everyone else around kept passing him, and I was the only one he was behind, so I pulled over. Detective Henry (fake name used to protect myself in the event of any future legal problems in the town) climbed out of his cruiser, took my license, and asked me what I was doing going almost twenty miles over the limit and passing on the right, which is apparently illegal, as I found out.

"Well, Officer," (I didn't notice Detective on his name plate until later), "since you asked, I'll tell you. I was diagnosed with multiple sclerosis yesterday and am on my way to my first treatment at Cape Cod Hospital and am running late. I'm a little overwhelmed and that is no excuse, I know, but there you go."

His face seemed to fall with concern. I still had the huge Bible-sized folder on the drug injections in the backseat to prove my unbelievable tale. He asked me my prognosis. He told me about a police officer he worked with who had to leave the force due to MS. He gave me tips that he and his fellow officers learned from their comrade. He advised me that it was important to stretch my muscles. I asked the officer's name. It turned out I knew the officer he was talking about. He had been on the Provincetown force with my father before going to Eastham.

"Is your father Freddy deSousa?"

"He is."

"Well, you definitely have a lot on your plate right now so I'm not going to give you a ticket. But slow down. And stretch your muscles."

Then he apologized for stopping me! If I had been out of the car, I swear he would have hugged me. I thanked him and drove off, going about thirty the whole rest of the way.

I was, of course, very late to the hospital. Checking in, I was directed to a sad, busy little unit I never knew existed, and introduced to the nicest, friendliest group of nurses I ever met. They plugged me up with the one hour long steroid infusion in the gentlest way possible, and chatted as they moved about the other patients, most of whom looked too used to being in the room. Many of the patients were clearly very sick and uncomfortable. Yet they smiled at the nurses, who made a point of talking to them, even teasing them to make them laugh as they assisted them with their infusions. The nurses teased me too, calling me a newbie. I didn't mind. I was a newbie. And needle or no, it was still a relief to sit down for an hour on an unplanned day off. I used the time to chat with some of the other patients and make more Christmas plans. I did not use it to think about why I was there.

Afterwards, I went to my hair appointment in the mall. I didn't desperately need this hair appointment, and who makes a hair appointment for the mall right before Christmas anyway? And who keeps it when they have just received overwhelming news and are having a difficult time trying to walk? But I went, because I didn't have to work that day, and I was thrilled that I didn't have to stay in the hospital. Suddenly I felt I had all the time in the world. There was hardly any parking at the mall, of course. But I managed to find one spot directly in front of a truck belonging to my new crush, a guy I found interesting and handsome and who I got tongue-tied and pathetically silly just thinking about. Seems on the Friday before Christmas, he had mall business too. There was no mistaking the vehicle. It was his.

I limped to my appointment looking all around me, drumming up visions of us bumping into each other and escaping the crowds for a holiday beverage. Or maybe him seeing my newly coiffed self and asking my help with buying presents. Or finding him searching for obviously female gifts for a girlfriend I didn't think he had. Or walking into him with this unknown girlfriend and tripping over my numb legs and making a fool of myself. None of those things happened. In fact, I never saw him there. When I was done with my haircut, his truck was still in front of my car. But now I was too tired to care. School girl fantasies were no match for multiple sclerosis and so I went home.

Checking messages later, I discovered a voicemail from a company asking me to call them. All I could hear on the message was something that sounded like "lifelines." The irony of this was too much. I called Laurie in a near panic. "What the hell is this? Is this the 'I've fallen and I can't get up' people who want me to call them? Am I now on some weird telemarketer list for the disabled that wants me to buy one of those special phones and bracelets? Nana had one of those! I am not Nana! There is no way I'm getting this, no way! This is crazy. How fast do these people work anyway? Can't I just breathe for a second before I have to start worrying about this crap?"

"Calm down dummy," she said, giggling. "It's MS Lifelines. They disperse the medication."

"Oh. Well, I guess that's better then." Feeling foolish, I jotted down the number. But still in avoidance mode, I stuck the paper with the phone number on top of my 'things to do pile' and instead of calling, turned on the TV, and channel surfed for Christmas specials.

You would think the next day I would rest, but I didn't. I went to the third infusion and then went to visit Anna, who was on bed rest, and whose baby shower I was going to miss the next day due to class and church. Then, as if I didn't have enough going on, I invited my mom and my Aunt Liliana to lunch just because my aunt was in town. What was I thinking? The last thing I had the energy to do was entertain. But I picked up some takeout sandwiches for us and hosted the impromptu lunch. Then I spent the late afternoon fielding calls from the parents of my students wondering what would happen to Sunday school considering the weather forecast predicted a huge snowstorm the next day. I was concerned about the storm too. I lived the furthest out of town (about half an hour), and would have the trickiest time getting to church. Plus, I was having a Mass said for Richard, my first love. He had not had a memorial service, and it seemed there should be some formal way to mark his passing. It was just a regular Mass where his name would be mentioned. It wasn't much to say goodbye but I felt it was the least I could do.

Now, with the storm coming and a full agenda, I was worried. Should I rent a hotel room overnight to be in town? How could I afford that now? Should I stay at a friend's house? Was I up to socializing that night? What if I stayed in town and couldn't get back? It always took hours, even days sometimes, to get my private road plowed and so I might not be able to get home. On and on the questions and minor worries in my brain went, adding to my exhaustion but at least not allowing me to think about what was making me so exhausted. It was easier to worry about how I'd get to Sunday School in a storm than what the hell my life was going to be like with MS.

In the end, I didn't go anywhere. The storm came and brought almost a foot of snow. Class was cancelled and there was no way

I was getting out of my road, or getting back in, had I left. I took Dora's advice and lit a candle and said special prayers for my friend Richard, sadly realizing that it was likely no one from his life was there to hear it when his name was said at Mass. But I watched the beautiful snow and finally got some of the rest I so desperately needed.

Leaving work the next morning for that day's infusion was tricky. I was already very behind from missing Friday and most of Thursday. And the roads were a mess. I had managed to get out of my private road, but skidded on the highway, almost causing a heart attack (like I needed another medical issue) and the drive from work to the hospital was terrifying. It was a short holiday week and that helped ease the tension work, messy roads, and infusions were causing. My mom and Drew had plans to come over the following evening to deliver presents and I told my mom that in my tricky driveway I was able to clear a place for my car only. Just to dig out the space my little Corolla needed was a long, cold, exhausting process. She and Drew would likely have to park down the road a bit if the snow didn't melt.

It bothered my mom that I had to worry about shoveling on top of everything else, so she called my dad, who was now back from Aruba, and told him how my driveway was a mess and with my diagnosis I really shouldn't be shoveling that much snow. As I left work for the holiday week on Tuesday, I listened to a very nice voicemail message from my dad, telling me not to worry about my driveway, he had fixed it for me. "Cool," I thought, "that is one less worry." I drove into my driveway and wasn't two inches in when I proceeded to get stuck. I backed out and got stuck again. I drove half an inch forward and got stuck again. It seems what my dad did to take care of my driveway was to drive over the already-plowed area to spread the snow around, making more room for parking—parking on inches of soft snow not compatible with anything but a four-wheel drive vehicle. Perhaps that is how they clear snow in Aruba. *Well, he tried,* I thought, as I grabbed the shovel to fix the driveway for good this time. When I told my mom how my dad had helped she wanted to know if she and Drew would be able to get in. "I don't know, Mom, Drew is a big kid. He'll figure it out."

The morning of Christmas Eve, I was excited. Christmas was here, I wasn't in the hospital and I was practically ready. I had just a few more gifts to wrap, a few treats to take out of the pan and divvy up among plates for the visits I would make later, shower, and go. Except the phone kept ringing with holiday well-wishers and last-minute plan-makers. I had showered and was in my warm, light blue, soft fuzzy bathrobe. It made me look like a huge blue bunny but it was comfy and good to wear while I did hair and makeup before getting dressed. UPS called to tell me they had a package for me but couldn't find me. Was it a surprise package from Zack? I was on hold for twenty minutes sorting out the address error and at the end of the call realized it was a package of information from the drug company. Information only, not even real drugs. At least drugs would have seemed worth the wait. But that bummer news reminded me that I never called the MS Lifelines people back and if I didn't do it now, I wouldn't be able to call them until the following week. I thought I had better get it over with; how long could it take?

I was on hold for another twenty minutes until I finally got the actual nurse I needed. And it turned out she needed to ask me twenty questions before she could send me the actual drugs. She proceeded to ask me every medical question under the sun for me, my siblings, my parents, my grandparents, my friends, my neighbors, past boyfriends, future boyfriends, etc.

In the middle of this inquisition, I saw a car pull up. It was Serena with her ten year old twins stopping by to wish me a Merry Christmas. Serena didn't know the MS news yet and I hardly ever got to see her girls. It was obvious I was home and I didn't want the kids to think I was ignoring them. I really wanted to see them, but I couldn't lose this call after I'd already put so much time into it! Without thinking, I answered the door, forgetting I was in the fuzzy blue bathrobe. While the nurse on the line was asking me questions in one ear, I was facing extreme hoots of laughter at my attire from not only Serena, but her tough-as-nails boyfriend, Bootsie, and receiving hugs and kisses from her daughters. The whole time the nurse was asking, "Do you lie out in the sun? Have you ever lied out in the sun? Does anyone you know lie out in the sun? Have you ever been to Africa? Has anyone you know ever been to Africa? Do you know where Africa is? Do you even like Africa?" In the bathrobe that was no longer so comforting, I tried to get the nurse to pause for a breath, explain to the girls why I couldn't invite them in and tell them where I dropped off their presents, and get Serena and Bootsie to pipe down without flipping them off as that wouldn't be appropriate for the day or the kids.

And like that, it was Christmas. Time for visiting and the beautiful Mass and family and it was all I hoped it would be, complete with new holiday memories. Like how my mom, who never drinks, got tipsy on one glass of wine, causing Drew and me to sprint to the parking lot to quickly get the car and get her home, leaving her swaying drastically with only Laurie and her Canadian crutch to try to keep her from falling over. Or, how, while chatting with them and making dinner on Christmas Day I missed the roasting pan and instead sprayed my entire kitchen floor with Pam, making my kitchen a makeshift ice rink for us all. Laurie and my mom were forbidden from stepping on the slippery floor, as I didn't want them to get hurt. But Drew and I had fun gliding around and serving while my mother watched nervously and waited for the plate-crashing display that never actually came. Drew managed some pretty nice spins while carrying the mashed potatoes and I was glad that my slide didn't turn into an awkward split. Silly memories maybe, but isn't that part of what the holidays are all about? And giggling with my family felt much better than focusing on my future with a chronic illness.

MYELIN MADNESS

During the weekend following the holiday, I was finally able to catch my breath and think for a bit. I bailed on a family event out of town, much to the chagrin of my impassioned Portuguese relatives who now wanted to bond more than ever. In their minds, I was going through something medically significant and they needed me to make the two-hour-plus drive to visit them so they could help me through it. I anguished over their hurt feelings and then said screw it, I need to process all of this. My favorite holiday was over and I had been diagnosed with multiple sclerosis.

The steroid infusions must have been working, because the random numbness and sporadic tingling had started to calm down. I no longer looked drunk when walking. And although I was more fatigued than ever, my legs seemed to be under control. It was time for me to really think about what this diagnosis would mean to my life.

From the years that Laurie had suffered through MS, I had learned a little about the illness. I no longer told people it was a muscle disease like I did for the first four years after Laurie's diagnosis. *A muscle disease? What was I thinking?* I'd been completely clueless, spreading misinformation about an illness that had nothing to do with hers.

I now knew it was a disease that affected one's nerve cells. But affected them how? I should have already understood this information, but alas, I had been forced to admit to Dr. M that even though my sister had been diagnosed eight years prior, I needed an MS refresher course. Dr. M. explained that protecting everyone's nerve cells is a substance called myelin. People with MS have certain immune cells in their system that attack this myelin, leaving the nerves exposed and causing all kinds of incredibly painful, terrifying, annoying and serious symptoms. Hmmm … That was a lot of stuff to think about that I wasn't sure I wanted to think about. I chose to let my mind wander instead.

The word myelin stood out and led my rambling brain back in time. Myelin, myelin … hmmm, sounds like Mylan. Through all twelve years of elementary and high school, I had in my class a boy named Mylan whom all the girls thought was handsome and cool. Every girl in the class would have gone out with him, had he asked.

How could Mylan be causing this kind of trouble in my body? I never got to go out with him. I may have kissed him during a Spin the Bottle game at Bootsie's one night, but I couldn't remember for sure. It may have been wishful thinking or maybe I kissed another good looking guy in our class. It might have been that

Mylan had kissed one of my best buddies instead. My memory of the party, and the fact that there was a lot of beer at that party, had distorted the image. Mylan and myelin sounded the same but the only thing they had in common was directing my mind away from what I didn't want to think about too much.

I forced myself to return to my crash course on multiple sclerosis. To help alleviate my confusion Dr. M had given me a book that showed a picture of a healthy nerve ending with this myelin stuff on it that I must say was nowhere near as good-looking as the high school heartthrob, Mylan. Lower on the page was the same diagram but now it had these critter looking things barreling out of a bunker-like blood vessel and forming a force field of some kind attacking this stuff. On the next page was the same picture but now the nerve cell looked all weak and wobbly and the myelin stuff had big chomps taken out of it. Since I had Mylan on the brain, and therefore was thinking of my high school years in the '80s, it occurred to me that the diagram looked like an evil version of PAC-Man. These buggy looking things in my body attacking the healthy looking things in there were causing me to lose points in the form of bizarre symptoms. I had never been good at PAC-Man, so it was quite troublesome.

The lesions they had found in my brain and on my spine were now useless clumps of this myelin stuff. It was just lying around taking up space in my already overwrought brain and being, well, useless.

To prevent confusion to the reader I should note that the guy, Mylan, is not a useless clump, last his fellow classmates knew. He hasn't posted any recent Facebook statuses about being assaulted and exposing anyone's nerve endings to viciously attacking cells, but you never can tell. I made a mental note to check with his wife.

Before I pulled out my yearbook and went further down memory lane, thus avoiding the immediate concern, I tried to focus. Back to the medical issue at hand. Dr. M explained that people with MS suffer different symptoms depending on where their particular attacks occur. She had given me the fancy book with the diagrams and freebies as she thought it might be helpful to have the specific description of MS and a complete list of the possible symptoms. The first thing the book said was that MS was an auto-immune disease, meaning that my body was attacking itself! *That was helpful,* I thought.

It was about as helpful as watching *Invasion of the Body Snatchers* when I was young. At the time, everyone was talking about puberty and all the changes my body would be going through. I had no idea what that meant. Then my body started to do all these weird and scary things, just like the movie! It freaked me out. What part of my body made another part so mad that it decided to launch an attack? The book said people with MS can suffer from the following: pain, balance problems, muscle stiffness, muscle spasms, walking issues, talking issues, weakness, bowel and/or bladder problems, difficulties with vision or vision loss, extreme fatigue, cognition and memory problems, depression, abnormal feelings and sensations, heat sensitivity, and not to be outdone, sexual issues. It did not say if the sexual issues were good sexual issues or bad sexual issues but I figured it was probably a good thing I was single.

All of this was so very intimidating and terrifying that it was no wonder my mind kept wanting to revisit high school—there was far less drama then. But I would have to deal with my feelings at some point, so I read on. Since I had relapsing-remitting MS, there was hope that I might stay where I was symptom-wise. It was possible that if I started shooting up the recommended medical cocktail on a regular basis I could possibly keep things from getting worse. In an attempt not to panic too much, I did the thing all wise people do. I turned to the internet for answers. I Googled "multiple sclerosis" and thousands of pages appeared. Where to begin? Facts, stats, stages, treatments, causes, symptoms, medicines, prognoses, diagnosis, doctors, therapies, books, pictures, pictures ... there was that vicious PAC-Man-looking diagram again.

I floundered a bit and then came upon a website that talked about something called the MS hug, a cruel and bizarre name if ever there was one. Laurie had mentioned a hug from time to time and I had assumed she was trying to tell me something about her boyfriend. Now I realized this was another symptom I had been experiencing for years that I just thought was a sign of my going crazy. Off and on for a while I would get this pain in my abdomen. In minutes it would sharply increase, then sharply decrease. The best I came up with to explain the stomachache was maybe my body was reacting badly to the fact that I had eaten some vegetables, another reason I should avoid them. I had no idea it was part of MS.

Looking back, there was more I could relate to on the list of symptoms. For years I worried that I would have early Alzheimer's disease as I was sometimes spacey and forgetful. One of my grandmothers had that horribly debilitating disease. I often worried that I was too young to forget what I was on my way to do in the few steps from the bedroom to the bathroom. When I told people about this memory loss, the standard response was, "Oh, I know. It's old age. I get that too." So I figured maybe they were right, I was just naturally spacey and the older I got, the worse I got. *Try not to worry*, I had told myself. *It couldn't be Alzheimer's. Nana Sousa was much older when she got it.* Now I realized it was part of the onset of MS.

Then I thought about the bladder issues. Very often, especially at night before I went to bed, I would have to pee six or seven times before falling asleep. I would really think I was done, there couldn't possibly be anymore left in there, and no sooner had I crawled back into bed, then I had to go again. And it wasn't in my mind, I really would go again. And again. The fact that I was a slight germaphobe with very dry hands led to a nightly ritual I would repeat on those nights over and over. Pee, wash my hands, put lotion on, go back to bed. Toss and turn for a few minutes while I tried to tell myself I DID NOT have to go again, it was all in my head. Then give up, head to the bathroom, pee again, repeat above. I checked the symptom list again—yup, bladder issues.

These things only happened sometimes and for fear of being seen as a hypochondriac at Mandy's office, and since they would often go away, it didn't seem worthy of mentioning. Then they would come back and I would wonder again if I should make an appointment. But now it all made sense and I didn't know if I should be relieved that I wasn't a hysterical lunatic or terrified of what all of this could mean for my future.

My mind was adrift in a sea of web information and memory overload. This is what I was reading and processing in the early days of the diagnosis, the days after Christmas and just before New Year's 2010. It seemed too weird to be true. But it was true. And it was time to accept and adjust.

SHUT UP MY HEAD

This sentence, "Shut up my head," doesn't make sense. Frankly, it isn't even a sentence. I don't know where it came from or what it is, but in the weeks after the holiday, as I was finally processing everything, this comment is what I would wake up to. It was a strong voice in my brain, shouting at me to *shut up my head*! I'll explain.

Saturdays were the only days I could sleep late and really rest. And I would sleep late; sleeping was far less of a problem than waking up was. But when I woke up, I would hear that voice in my head. It may have come from the headaches, the bizarre constant dreams that someone who spends ten hours in deep REM sleep comes up with, the well-intentioned yet overwhelming advice from everyone, or the new list of things to do. It may have come from all those things combined, just rolling around in my overly fatigued brain. I had gone from purposely not thinking about MS, to thinking about it all the time, and I was overwhelmed. All I wanted to do was *shut up my head*! Perhaps the best way to get rid of the obnoxious voice was by adjusting to and accepting all the things that were swirling around my brain. So that is what I set out to do.

First up in my "adjusting and accepting list" was learning to administer the new meds. At the time, these MS medications were only available in injection form and were designed to help keep the illness where it was, slowing or stopping the progression. There was no medication to reverse the damage already caused, but there were several proven drugs that could reduce flares and exacerbations and generally slow it down. As Laurie helpfully pointed out, the injections I chose had the words "Chinese hamster ovary cells" written on the box. What was that about? Why Chinese hamsters? And why their ovary cells? What scientist was hanging out in his lab and came up with the idea to put ovary cells in an MS drug? The Portuguese hamster's liver cells didn't do anything and the Italian hamster's lung cells are useless. I know, let's try Chinese hamster ovary cells. No one seemed to be able to explain it to me so after a while, I stopped thinking about it too much.

I had met with Nancy, the friendly nurse, who came to my house to show me how to administer the shots. They were a major drag and I don't care what anyone says, they stung. A lot. Especially the thigh ones. Why is that? Since I was a kid my thighs have always been thunderous and you would think all the extra fat would cushion the sudden stab of the twelve-inch needle shot out instantly from the auto-injector.

OK, the actual needle was barely one quarter of an inch, but it sure seemed bigger. I would hold the injector to the designated area for ten minutes while I talked myself into pushing the button.

Responsible me: *Just push the button and be done with it.*

Wimpy me: *No, I don't want to push the button, it's gonna hurt.*

Responsible me: *You have to push it, so just get it over with.*

Wimpy me: *Why do I have to push it, why don't I just push it later?*

Aggravated responsible me: *JUST PUSH THE DAMN BUTTON!*

When I needed to yell at myself it always made me think that the patients who did the shots without the injector (like Laurie) and those who had to do the muscle shots were just heroic. How much encouraging self-talk did you have to employ to purposely stab a really large needle deep into the muscles of your own body?

The thirty-second auto-injector shot was actually an all-day process. I would take the shot out of the fridge first thing in the morning, as it was supposed to be stored in the fridge but administered at room temperature. When it was time to do the shot at night I would take a pain reliever, wash my hands even if I had done so previously because the directions said you had to, and then hold it in my hand for five minutes, as instructed by Nancy. Since I would get bored in the five minutes, I would usually start playing solitaire on the computer while I waited for it to reach the exact warmth of my hand, as recommended by the pharmacy folks in the know. Since I stink at solitaire and am adamant about winning, I would usually wind up holding the thing for twenty minutes while I tried to beat the computerized cards.

When I finally gave up on the game and remembered the task at hand, I would check my prescription notebook for where on my body I should do the shot this time. According to Nancy, it was important to rotate the injection sites (butt cheeks, thighs, fleshy part of the upper arms and tummy). I worried that if I didn't rotate exactly as I was told to, something horrible would happen. The shot could blow up or maybe the world would collapse. Perhaps by revolving injection sites precisely, I was sending positive MS vibes out into the medical and drug communities. If I had to do this, the perfectionist in me was determined to do it right. I became addicted to the drug notebook, studying it for several minutes and pulling out a ruler to measure the distance from the bruises of the previous sites. Far be it from me to mess up this part of the process.

Back to the injector and the shot itself where the needle needed to be uncapped and the injector launcher loaded and prepared to fire. Then it was time to hold a hot compress to the planned area for several minutes. Next, the alcohol swab for thirty seconds. But now, the area of my skin I was due to attack wasn't warm anymore so I would do the compress yet again. Then I would stress, wondering if the alcohol swab was now no longer useful and debating whether I should swab the area a second time. I would tell myself to move on and hold the auto-injector to the injection site. And that is when wimpy me and responsible me would start their regular argument about pushing the button.

After I finally did push the button, it was time for the two minutes of massaging the skin to disperse the medication. Then the warm compress again. Then the cleanup. Then I would realize I had actually done the shot an hour later than I had noted in my book and I would have to change that. By that point I was so exhausted that I would pass out, relieved I didn't have to do this regimen again for a couple of days.

Many times I would hit the button and nothing would happen—no sting at all and I would think, *wow, that one was easy,* only to realize that, in my exhaustion and fretting, I hadn't uncapped the needle. Thus the entire process would have to begin all over again. Apparently, for some insane reason, the drug doesn't work if you don't uncap the needle first.

Author's note: The above is what you get when you take an anal-retentive OCD-driven freak and give her an MS diagnosis!

One of the things I had to "shut up my head" about was the whining over having to actually do the shots. Around this time, a friend's nephew suddenly became very sick at school, was hospitalized with type II diabetes even though he had always been super healthy, and would now face a complete lifestyle change, including three shots a day! He was ten. He cried about having to do the shots for a whole hour. Then he was over it. I was so moved by this that even though I hadn't met him, I bought him some sports books my friend said he liked and wrote out a long rambling card about how I admired his courage and thought he was very brave and cool. When he received my present and the card, he probably guessed I was an old lady nutcase. But he sent a sweet thank you email anyway and even if he did think I was crazy, I still admired him and decided I wouldn't complain about the shots ever again. That is, unless I ever got literally stuck with the harder ones.

The phrase "shut up my head" that kept blasting from my skull came from other things too. Now it seemed there was a constant to-do list in my mind. In an effort to let go of all that was going in and out of my overtaxed brain, I made a 'to-do' list on paper. The writing of which just became another thing I needed to do. It looked something like this:

Call the insurance company

Return MS Lifelines call

Make sure I am registered at the National MS Society for information on what's going on

Order more shots

Call in new prescriptions

Schedule my primary appointment

Note when to schedule lab work

Email St. E's on progress

Read all the drug literature

Ask the drug company to send me the free pen and magnifying glass they forgot to put in my drug book

Read the pamphlets I picked up from St. E's

Read the book about women with MS that I had given Laurie when she was diagnosed that she had now given back to me

Search for chat rooms on MS

Search for support groups locally and online

Start exercising

Look for healthy recipes

Etc.

It seemed to just go on and on and I was always adding to the list. And then there were the regular things I needed to do too like pay bills, laundry, clean, gas up the car, grocery shop, and prepare for Sunday school. But all I wanted to do was sleep. I wanted to sleep on my lunch break. I wanted to sleep when I came home from work. I wanted to sleep on Saturdays. I wanted to sleep on Sundays when I got home from church and class.

I had started telling family and friends I didn't regularly see, and in their kind, supportive way they had lots of overwhelming advice for my already overwhelmed brain:

Write down how your meds make you feel

Write down when you have your symptoms and when you don't

Write down the times of the day when your symptoms are at their worst

Write down when you have the most energy

Write down when you have no energy

Write everything down

Read Montel's first book

Read Montel's last book

Read all of Montel's books

Read this book on fighting fatigue

Or read this book on taking proper vitamins

Hell, read them both

Take vitamin D

Make sure you don't take too much vitamin D

Always check your vitamin D levels

Try alternative medicine

Stretch your muscles (thank you Eastham Police Department)

Try yoga

If you try yoga, make sure it is a good program

Make sure you have something to support yourself with when doing yoga

Try massage

Whatever you do, don't do massage

Try acupuncture

Don't try acupuncture

Get a pet—they promote healing

Don't get a pet—they are too much work

Wear sunscreen always—sunscreen is very important

Don't wear sunscreen—you need to get vitamin D naturally

Drink lots of water, at least eight glasses a day

Drink green tea

Drink energy drinks

Drink energy drinks with green tea

Drink milk (this is a whole lot of drinking and it doesn't even include wine! Doesn't anyone understand about the bladder issues associated with MS?)

Eat vegetables

Don't eat corn—it has too much starch

Only buy organic vegetables

Don't waste money on organic, it is all the same

Wash fruit and veggies thoroughly, good to get a brush and veggie cleaning product

Just rinse produce, it's fine

Drink fruit juice to get in a serving of fruit and veggies

Don't drink fruit juice as it has too much sugar

Don't eat too much sugar

Don't eat aspartame

Eat agave nectar instead of sugar

Don't eat agave nectar

Take Ginkgo biloba

Don't take Ginkgo biloba (according to Laurie, if you can re-member how to say it, you don't need it)

Eat right

Take flaxseed

Eat bee pollen (What?)

Exercise

Try to balance out all the things you have to do

Thank goodness you don't have a pet, imagine all the work and expense

Begin thinking about what you want to do

Think how you want your day to go so you can conserve your day's energy

Don't waste your energy by thinking

Try not to do too much

Rest

It was all good advice and it all came from caring people, many in the know. I took it—well the last two anyway. I would get so tired that I would decide the best advice was the resting and not doing too much. So that is what I did. But my head still kept swirling with all I should be doing even as my body would say screw it all, except the resting part.

The lists of what I needed to do right away and what I should start doing when I was able didn't even begin to include the money worries. I was more convinced than ever that I needed to save money as my medical bills skyrocketed. Even with insurance it costs a lot to be poked, smashed, electrocuted, injected, and shipped down a narrow tube with your skull locked in a vise-like grip. I was constantly counting: counting change, counting my hours at work, counting my savings, and counting my bills. I became obsessed with concerns such as:

I found a dime on the sidewalk. Should I put it in my wallet or in my Lion's Pennies for Sight jar?

Should I rob from Peter to pay Paul? How much interest is Paul paying these days anyway?

Speaking of Peter and Paul, how much money should I put in the basket at church every week?

If I have a Mass said for my grandparents, shouldn't I have one said for my great aunt and uncle too? Is it too cheap of a donation to have them said together?

Should I plan on getting my religious education students a little gift at the end of the program? If so, what can I get them that is cheap and religious but not too silly or corny?

Cousin so-and-so's birthday is coming up. Should I go to Hallmark and buy a $2.99 card or just look and see if I have a good enough one hanging around? Do I have any greeting card coupons?

The co-pays on the injections are expensive. Should I go to China and get my own hamsters? Maybe I could breed Chinese hamsters and make some extra money selling them to other people with MS.

On and on it went. I would take my mom's used magazines (no way I was spending $4.99 at the cash register for my own new ones) and read the articles on how to save. But most of the suggestions were ones I was already doing. Borrow books and movies from the library for free, check. Get rid of the landline, check. Combine trips to save gas and fill up at the cheapest places, check. Cut coupons, check. I couldn't stop counting and thinking and worrying to the point of becoming completely rattled and since I wasn't shutting up my head, the only thing I decided I could do was crawl under the covers and put a pillow over my ears to somewhat quiet all the racket.

THE THINGS YOU DO ON SPEED

Physically I wasn't doing that badly. Since I had undergone one week of steroid infusions, the balance issues, numbness and tingling were mostly gone. They would visit occasionally, just to make sure I remembered them, but they were no longer a real problem. Otherwise, on really bad days, I had what I started to call the achy, shaky, spacey blues. My whole body would ache like it would ache when you had the flu, and not just after the shots like the pamphlets said they might. It occurred to me that this happened a lot in the years before the diagnosis. So many times I would feel as though I was about to be floored by a nasty bout of the flu. Zack would bring me toast or soup in bed, and would make me his disgusting hot toddy which he swore cured all. I would drink it only out of appreciation for the fact that he had made it for me. The nastiness would go away and I would be convinced it was due to the drink. I never actually got the flu so what else could we think? My sister never had this symptom and so the only other explanation seemed to be that I was losing my mind. The hot toddy cure-all theory seemed the safest bet. Now that there was a real explanation for the aches, and since Zack had taken his recipe with him and it really was disgusting, I decided the reason the toddy helped was that it was made for me and brought to me in bed. It doesn't have the same healing power if you make it yourself.

There were also frequent, horrible headaches and whoever happened to invest in Aleve during that time is very rich today. Sometimes I would feel shaky, not quite in control, not totally secure on my feet and my hands and fingers would be a little unsteady if I was holding something. And there was spaciness. I had always been a space shot, but within reason. The reason would be when I wanted to be goofy with my friends or Zack or when there was just a lot on my mind. It was a fun spaciness. Now it was spaciness whenever it just felt like showing up and it was getting tricky to handle. This spaciness made it hard to concentrate on any but the simplest of tasks. Sometimes my mind felt like it was in a fog and what little brain cells I had tossing around in my head had to sort through the fog. 2+2 equals 4—easy. But 2+2+4-3, no way. That I would need to rest on. Or, grab a calculator. There were also strange earaches and noises in my ear and sometimes I would get a sudden spasm of pain like I was being stabbed. It would last for about thirty seconds and then go away. Just plain weird ...

But this was all fairly manageable and considering what I knew of the symptoms of other patients, including my own sister, I felt pretty lucky. I wasn't in constant pain or facing issues that were causing me to have trouble walking. I wasn't falling down and my vision was still sharp. What was doing me in was the extreme exhaustion. It had increased, and my life consisted of going to work, coming home and catching up with my friends on the phone for a bit, and then asleep by eight, sometimes even by seven. Then I would get up and do it all again until Friday, when we usually ended work at noon. Errands, family visits, and preparing for Sunday school would be done Friday afternoon. Saturday, I would rest. Sunday I would go to church and class and then come home and rest some more and start again on Monday. There was no going out at night unless I had a Lion's meeting—and if I expended the energy to go to a meeting, then I would pay for it with even more exhaustion until the weekend. I quit a domestic violence committee I was on as those meetings were also at night, and it was just too much. Most of the time, all that rest was not enough and the fatigue just became unbearable. I was frustrated because I felt too exhausted to do the simplest tasks. Standing at the sink to do dishes could make me want to cry. You don't really think about the energy it takes to wash a glass or two until you no longer have the energy to do it. Sometimes just lifting my arm to brush my teeth was too much. Tasks at work that I usually excelled at were often left undone or done poorly. It seemed like it took great effort to do one small errand and then I would need to rest before continuing with the other.

I called the nurses at St. E's and told them what was going on. They discussed my fatigue with Dr. M and she prescribed what the nurses called a stimulant. My friends called it legal speed. Once the prescription was called in I needed to wait for the insurance company to approve it. When they finally did, I got a letter from them saying they would only approve a thirty day supply. *So*, I thought, *I will just be conservative about taking it, no big deal.* But then I picked it up and the bottle said I needed to take it every day. So I was supposed to take one a day for a month, get the relief I needed, and then go back to my old , 'so tired the thought of just brushing my teeth makes me want to weep' ways?

I called the pharmacy and asked how much the drug cost once insurance stopped covering it. The pharmacist said I didn't want to know; it was so expensive there was no way I could cover it. Since he really didn't know me or my finances and didn't know if I was actually a lottery winner or not, I figured it must be pretty bad. I slept on this. And slept. And slept some more. I finally called my insurance company and indignantly, with the letter in front of me, I demanded to know how they could approve a medication I desperately needed for one month only? I had a bit of a 'tude with the poor agent, as I was frustrated beyond belief.

"Ma'am, we only approve this medication once per thirty days, you can renew it after the thirty day period."

"No, it says right here, only allowed one refill in thirty days."

Then I stopped and sheepishly apologized. Apparently I was too tired to read the letter accurately. To keep me from going to a street corner and selling the stuff, only one refill at a time was allowed. Made perfect sense to someone who was actually awake.

The first time I was able to start the medication was on Valentine's Day. It wasn't planned that way. But we didn't have class that day due to the school break and I had gone to the Saturday vigil Mass so I would be home that Sunday. There were warnings everywhere about not driving when you are on it and making sure you are in a safe place in case you freak out. Plus, I had a lot I needed to do. Valentine's Day or no, it seemed like a good day to try it. Laundry had drastically piled up and the house needed a good cleaning. Usually I tried my best to honor the fourth commandment but with all that was going on, this seemed like the only time to get these things done and I hoped God would forgive—certainly I'd done enough resting other days. I also had a new recipe I wanted to try, an adult healthy version of my favorite comfort food—macaroni and cheese. OK, so, on its own, it wasn't necessarily the best in healthy options but at least I could start with baby steps.

The other thing on my mind that weekend was an exercise plan I thought I would actually do. I had recently tried my friend Lynn's Nintendo Wii Fit system. I went through the whole setup with her daughters and brother, while the system told me how out of control obese and disgusting I was and how I desperately needed to shape up. Lynn and her girls weighed about 100 pounds altogether. Once I got through that humiliation, I really enjoyed it. I had fun playing the games and thought it was a workout I would do regularly. Her kids showed me some of their favorites, and I wasn't too bad at them. Since I refused to spend money on a gym membership knowing I wouldn't go anyway, Wii Fit seemed to be for me. As they were fairly new to the market, they were extremely popular. I went to the local electronics megastore and was told they were sold out. The only way I could get a Wii Fit system was to get up incredibly early on Sunday morning, check the newspaper flyer, and if one was listed in the flyer then come directly to the store and wait for them to open. Yeah, right.

That Valentine's Day Sunday morning, I took the speed (oops, sorry, *prescription stimulant*), and started the laundry and pulled the bathroom apart for a complete scrub down. One hour into the drug I thought about the Wii and called the store. They had received a shipment and had eleven in stock. No, they could not hold them even if you used your credit card to purchase it over the phone. I really wanted one but had laundry in the washer and the dryer, scented candles lit, and hadn't even taken a shower. It was Cape Cod in the middle of winter, how fast could they possibly go? I didn't feel any different from the new drug in my system and decided to finish what I was doing.

At 1:30 I called the store again thinking that if they had sold a few, I might jump in the shower and head up. If not, I would wait until after work the next day. They had one left and no, they couldn't hold it. "Please," I begged, "I am thirty-five minutes away." But no, not even with plastic and a huge tip.

I debated. There was still laundry in, I still hadn't showered and was now really skanky. If ten Wii systems actually went that quickly, there was no way I was going to make it in time to get the last one. I gave up and went down to the basement to put the final load in the dryer. In that second, I think the pill was officially kicking in, because I decided to go for it. I shut the dryer off, blew out the candles, grabbed my pocketbook and coat and hit the road in sweats and with unbrushed hair. I forgot all about not driving until you are familiar with the effects of the drug. I was on a mission and headed up Cape. That last Wii was mine.

I got stuck behind an elderly couple on a Sunday drive on the mid-Cape one-lane express. My sister called and I told her what I was doing and how I couldn't get past these folks to get my Wii. She suggested I beep the horn, roll down the window, and if I shouted loud enough they might get the message to pull over since a Wii system was very important. They didn't.

When I could I sped by them and took every shortcut I could possibly imagine, landing at the store in thirty-two minutes. And they were out of the Wii shipment. I asked two clerks. They both checked. They were gone. They directed me over to Thomas who they said might be able to help me. Thomas checked too, nope, none of the eleven were left. He called other stores off the Cape to see if they had any. That would be quite a hike but I was committed now. No, they didn't have any either. Thomas told me the best thing to do was to get up early Sunday morning and check the flyer and ..." Yeah, yeah, yeah. I've heard.

I looked around, in full-speed mode now. The sales flyer advertised that if you bought a Toshiba laptop computer for $399 you would get a free printer. I didn't have a computer and just went to the library when I needed one. I had thought about getting one eventually and since I was here, I might as well take a look. Before I knew what was happening, I bought one. And since I was on speed and have no clue about computer anything, I bought all the extras they told me to buy, including those warrantees I never agree to. I don't even know what I bought but I did know that my $399 computer was now actually costing me $1,200 but it was okay because I could pour a can of diet coke on the keyboard and the store would have to replace it. Since I didn't plan to pour a diet coke onto the keyboard all the extras were probably unnecessary but hey, what could I say, I was on speed.

They sent me back to the ever-helpful Thomas to do the financing and I asked him to throw in a Wii with my purchase. He laughed and said, "Isn't it funny how popular they are now? I can't even get rid of mine."

Me: "Say what?"

Him: "I am trying to sell mine 'cause I use my X-box more."

Me: "I'll buy it. How can I buy it?"

He only wanted one hundred dollars for it and said he would throw in the six games he bought and the battery charger for the remotes. A rational person would probably say this may not be wise, if it was broken I have no recourse, etc. But I did it anyway. After setting up my clandestine deal with Thomas and applying for a store credit card to pay for the laptop, I went home and finished my laundry, cleaned my bathroom, ironed my clothes for the week, showered, talked to four of my friends on the phone, and at eight, started my new recipe. I was usually in bed by eight on a Sunday and wasn't much of a cook, but here I was. During the cooking I set one of my potholders on fire, burnt my hand and sliced open a finger, but the dinner at 10:30 PM was delicious.

The next day after work I picked up my computer and Thomas generously helped me carry it out to my car, and then told me to drive to the side of the building where his car was. I did and gave him one hundred dollars and he gave me a perfectly good Wii and six games which I later sold for forty dollars. In one day I was now taking narcotics and making potentially shady back alley deals.

Thomas didn't have the Wii Fit board and disc set up so I spent the next couple of weeks looking everywhere for it in stores and online, and then in desperation emailing Nintendo a sob story about how I had recently been diagnosed with MS and how much it would help me with balance and weight loss issues but I couldn't find it anywhere. The day after emailing them I happened to be near a local Walmart I had already checked five or six times and thought I would check again. The new shipment had just arrived; my Wii Fit was complete. Over the next several days Nintendo repeatedly called and emailed to see how they could help. Good to know they were responsive! Between this and the speeding ticket I avoided the day after my diagnosis, Laurie said I had learned to play the MS card. I thought that was a little crass. I wasn't trying to be manipulative. What was true was true but hey, if I happened to mention it at a time when it would help me out, why not?

The pill was a miracle drug. I didn't notice it having any effect on my ability to drive or to perform my job. Perhaps my judgment wasn't the best, as evidenced by my $1,200 impulse-purchase computer, but I was happier and way more alert. For three days. Then it wore off and I was as fatigued as before. At thirty dollars a month while I was trying to save every penny (ignoring the new computer and extras of course), I decided to stop taking it. The next time I saw Dr. M and told her how the effects of the pill wore off after a few days, she told me I could ignore the dosage instructions and just take as needed. I was hesitant but just in case, kept a couple on me in a little pill box I kept in my pocketbook (yes, I had now advanced to carrying around a pill box, but at least hadn't gotten to the days of the week super box yet.)

One Tuesday I was dragging beyond belief after lunch and still had four more hours of work. The boss was gone and it would be quiet so I was looking forward to making a dent in my huge pile of work. But I was so exhausted I was probably more likely to fall asleep at my desk than actually do anything. On top of work, I wanted to stay awake because that night on *American Idol* the potential idols would all be singing Rolling Stones songs. I love the Stones. I had seen them in concert six times, mostly with Lynn, who was even more of a fan than I was. I had to stay awake to harshly condemn the contestants for daring to put their own take on a Jagger/Richards masterpiece, or to commend them for a respectable tribute. I took the drug and, while I don't remember what was accomplished that afternoon, I had much less work on my desk when I stumbled in the next morning.

However, here is what I did between 8:00 and 10:00 that evening: I did my dishes, I watched the show, I texted Lynn after each performance to review it, I spoke to Lynn about each performance on the phone, I spoke to my Mom to again try to point out the wonders of the Stones catalog, I watched the Bruins game, I texted my friend and fellow Bruins fan Kristin about each play in the game, I played Solitaire on my new computer, I brushed my teeth and I talked to Mya at length about the appeal argument on a case that was frustrating her, all simultaneously. I was even able to sleep that night and before I drifted off only seconds after hitting the pillow, it occurred to me again how amazing this little pill was.

That is, until I could barely get up the next day and was even worse off than I had been before taking the pill. I spent the rest of that week shuffling through my world in a zombie-like state. I grunted greetings to patients and stumbled around, tripping over the waste baskets, misfiling charts and disconnecting calls instead of answering them.

I was about to give up when my mom recommended that I cut the pill in half and try that. So one day when I was struggling again, I took a knife and fought with the thing until I managed to cut it in two. (I have since progressed to a fancy little pill splitter with my pharmacy's name on it which I was very excited to get for free, being a frequent customer and all.) I tried the half dose and didn't feel any difference at all. It was then that I gave up for good and thus ended my legal speed experiment.

GOD-GIVEN SMACK

With all of the commotion in my mind, it continued to be difficult to focus on the task at hand without letting myself get distracted by disruptive thoughts. It wasn't only me worrying about the brain clutter. God was starting to get pretty ticked off about where my mind wandered as well.

One extremely cold Sunday morning in February, I was on my way to teach my religious education class. I was prepared and on time, until I was intercepted by a fellow parishioner. She needed me to correct a mistake she had made on some program paperwork. This correction involved crossing out the mistake, re-writing the actual information on each sheet, and then passing out the paperwork to students in three classes. Somehow, it became my problem that her job wasn't done earlier. I wasn't thrilled by the assignment, the extra precious minutes of class time it would take, or frankly, the way she casually directed *me* to do it.

Carrying my books, coffee, and this unclasped bunch of papers, I scrambled to get to the classroom, angry cursing taking place in my head. I was aggravated by this woman and I wanted her to know it. Perhaps if I conjured up subliminal nasty messages they would reach her in the form of the stinkeye I was sending out as I hurried away. I would have stuck out my tongue, but I'm a loving Christian after all. And it was really, really cold in that parking lot.

Next thing I knew, I was down on the ground. Coffee was splashed all directions, and books and papers scattered everywhere. As I landed on my knees, what came out of my mouth was a loud "Fuck!" I didn't mean for that word to come out of my mouth, but I didn't mean to hit the ground either. I had no idea where the fall or the expletive outside of the church came from. I had no inclination of either until I was down.

Some people may say it was the gravel walkway that caused the fall, walking on rocks being difficult for even the most agile of folks. Laurie outright blamed MS: "Why beat yourself up? Why not just blame this sucky disease?" My stepmother blamed my new Shape Up shoes. A friend of hers who had the same shoes fell suddenly and broke her ankle. I didn't want it to be my new sneakers. They were so comfy, like walking on a cloud, and they were going to help me get fit. No one can blame ice—aside from the rapid crystallization the coffee was doing, there was no ice anywhere.

What occurred to me was that the fall might have been God giving me a little smack. What business did I have walking in to teach His children about His wondrous love with such malicious thoughts in my mind, especially over trivial things?

I didn't have time to sort it out, I had to recover and get to class. Step 1: Did anyone hear me, especially students? No kids had arrived yet and though the early Mass had begun, I didn't see any latecomers. The opening hymn was being played loudly enough to drown out my very un-teacher like and un-Christian like exclamation. No one had heard me. God is merciful in so many ways! Step 2: Damage control. My knee hurt and there was a hole in my favorite pair of jeans with a little bit of blood coming out. No gushes, just a scrape. A scrape I could hide while I taught. The coffee was a lost cause, but the cup had to be gathered so as not to add littering to my list of sins. The papers were flying all over the parking lot.

As I did my best to start collecting them, I looked up and saw an amazing sight. No, not a vision from heaven. Not a sign from above, at least not that I could tell at the time. (Although Laurie felt that due to the extreme unusualness of the location of this vision, it must have been some sort of a sign.) My dad had just pulled up in his truck. What was so unusual about that was the fact that my dad didn't go to church, ever. Maybe on extremely rare occasions like a funeral, and sometimes not even then. He hadn't witnessed the fall, but he was watching me crawl around the parking lot trying to pick up over thirty pieces of paper.

"Yvonne, why did you drop your papers?"

I grabbed what I could and stumbled over, thinking, *I don't know, I was bored, thought it might be fun.*

"I dropped them when I fell," I said.

"You fell? Why did you fall?" He asked loudly, in his Portuguese accent.

"I don't know, Dad—blame MS, blame it on me being a klutz. I don't know."

I was not about to explain the God-smacked-me theory, as I didn't think he would buy it. Something about seeing my dad at such an unexpected time was making me get teary. *Oh no,* I thought. *This is not going to happen. I have to teach class in five minutes and I have to get my act together.*

But my dad wanted to chat. So we did, with the minutes ticking away, and me trying not to cry, while checking my knee for any more blood that the older kids would use to delay class and the younger ones would be freaked out at. The kids were starting to arrive now, but since my dad had pulled into the area illegally (I told you, not a regular churchgoer so he didn't know the parking area too well) his truck was blocking the church's access way. The parents couldn't move forward with him blocking their path, and with others trying to drop off their kids, no cars could really back up. He had planned to drive the wrong way through the churchyard but with the parents' arrival, and the lot being full, he had a bit of a maneuver to get his truck turned around. It bought me a few extra minutes. I used the precious time to pull myself together and try to get the paper mess sorted out.

Days later I thought to ask him what he was doing there, how he happened to be in the church lot that morning, a place he would never usually go.

"I wanted to have coffee with my buddy Fuzzy, and sometimes that crazy bastard goes to church, so I was looking for him."

"Oh, I guess that makes sense." I was reminded of where my knack for cursing came from.

The weird thing was, I remembered another time when my dad showed up at church unexpectedly, just when I needed his help. Five years earlier, the church building had burned to the ground the day after a major blizzard. The volunteer fire department had to tread through snow thigh-deep to fight the fire, but there wasn't much they could do. Parishioners were absolutely devastated, me included. We couldn't imagine recovering from the loss and we all came to the spot to share our misery. Once the fire officials said the area was safe, we stood in the parish hall to weep, pray, and share our memories. We were in awe that no one was hurt, and that most of the altar, including the tabernacle was spared, even though the roof had collapsed.

Many of us tried to get close to the building to survey the damage. Between the snow from the blizzard and the cold that froze the water used to fight the fire, the frozen ground was very slippery. I wasn't really thinking clearly; with tears in my eyes, I decided to walk to the front of the church and make sure the Fatima shrine wasn't destroyed too. I couldn't ask the firefighters; they were still busy, and I needed to see it for myself.

The church, or what was left of it, was situated on a steep hill. As I walked to the front, the hill was now covered by a sloping sheet of ice. There was no way I could walk back up it to get to the safer lot area. To go forward meant sliding on my butt into traffic where drivers weren't really paying attention as they were crying at the sight of the destroyed building. I was stuck. A truck cautiously pulled up alongside of me. The driver rolled down the window and asked, "What are you doing? Don't you know it's dangerous walking around out there?" It was my dad, out for a ride, and checking things out for himself. Even though he didn't go to Mass, the church was still in his heart and in his history. I got in and he drove us around a couple of times to understand all that had happened and to see that the beloved shrine was intact. Then he took me back to my car. Our parish did recover but it took great love, faith, prayers, donations, and more tears.

So Laurie had to be right—there must have been a reason my dad showed up right after that fall. God must have had a plan. Maybe he was there to stall long enough so I wouldn't break down in front of my class. Who knows? But I still couldn't help thinking the fall was God giving me a push to remind me what was important, and what was unnecessary. He wanted me to get rid of the garbage in my brain.

I had always been a klutz, before and after the diagnosis, but I usually knew what dumb move I had made to cause it. The dumb move here was that at the same time I was planning on showing the kids how much I loved God, I was in my head cursing out a fellow Christian. God didn't appreciate it and wanted to let me know. Just a little shove of a reminder to throw off my resentments and negativity. I did believe in loving one another and putting others first. I also believed in forgiveness and helping others whenever and however possible. Yet I still became too easily focused on annoyances I perceived as personal. How could my beliefs get so easily thrown out the window when I felt slighted? Perhaps the bigger lesson was I should worry less about the huge tumor-looking lesion in my brain, and more about the black cloud I sometimes allowed to color my heart.

Great, add that to the list of things I needed to work on. I should probably put this at the top of the list. Well, at least the veggies got moved down on the list again—yay!

Author's note:
Within a year of that fall, my dad started attending church weekly with his buddy, that crazy bastard Fuzzy. After Mass they go out for coffee. God does work in mysterious ways.

IT'S A
MYSTERY TO ME

It was March now. I was still tired. And I was more obsessed with money concerns than ever. I had never been cheap and was actually pretty generous when giving money to others, maybe too much so. But my diagnosis had me worrying about everything in my future, including my finances. I continued to panic about the increasing cost of medical co-pays and wanted to pad my savings as much as possible. And my savings wasn't the only padding stressing me out. I wasn't losing any weight as exhaustion was dragging me down, and I hardly ever exercised.

It didn't help that Thomas, the helpful computer department guy, had sold me a used, sarcastic Wii. After agreeing with Lynn's Wii that I was disgusting and had A LOT of work to do, my used Wii felt that calling me on my faults would be the best get fit medicine. If I missed a day of working out (or two or five or ten), my Wii would greet me with, "Is that you, Yvonne? So nice to see you. It has been a zillion days since your last work out." Or, "Hello Yvonne, where have you been? I missed you. Are you ready for a really big workout?"

Maybe I should have taken comfort in the fact that at least someone was missing me, even if it was a computer in my TV, but I always just assumed the animated voice had a secret agenda. At least it wasn't just me, my Wii was sarcastic to Drew, too. Drew had set up the system, making himself a little Mii before moving to Arizona with his girlfriend. One day the Wii asked if I noticed him developing any love handles since he wasn't working out. *Ha ha*, I thought, *at least the Wii is hard on Drew too.* But the next time I turned it on it had the nerve to tell me that maybe the reason Drew wasn't working out was because I wasn't paying enough attention to him! Apparently the Wii assumed Drew and I were a couple, which if that wasn't so sick would have been flattering as Drew was less than half my age, and according to the Wii, had an "excellent physique."

Now, if you didn't jump on the Wii craze yourself, you may require some explanation here. The Miis were onscreen characters that could interact with the Mii you made of yourself. As you move, your Mii moves on screen. Some games on the system required you and your Mii to interact with other little Miis. The Miis in the system were stressing my Mii out. Whenever I tried to hula hoop, Drew's Mii whipped the hoops at my Mii so fast she would be knocked out. And when my Mii would do the basic step aerobics game, in the rare circumstances when she got several perfect scores in a row, the other Miis would smile at her encouragingly, but it was only an act. Their smiles were actually a secret plot to break her concentration and make her miss the next several steps.

I kicked butt or, actually balls, in the soccer head butt game, in spite of the Drew Mii trying to dive bomb the me Mii with helmets and sneakers. I texted Drew, "YOUR MII IS AGGRAVATING MY MII ON THE WII!" Drew's response, "WAY TO GO LITTLE MII! LOL"

I couldn't even rely on my Wii yoga and strength trainer. I had picked the female Wii Mii (or if it was a trainer, was it a Yuu? I never knew). I didn't need more stress trying to do yoga moves in front of a guy, even if he was an animated one. So I worked with the woman on the system and tried not to wonder too much about how and why she changed her hairstyle from time to time, until one day I turned on the system and the guy was there. He said he would be working with me that day. Who says? Where does an animated girl instructor go and why? Did I tire her out? Did she need a vacation? Was she doing yoga in Aruba? How come my computerized yoga girl gets a vacation but I don't? These questions tired me out even more and seemed excuse enough to turn away from the Wii for a bit and shift my focus yet again.

So what was I to do about my other concern, money? I turned to the new $1,200 computer I didn't really need. I became obsessed with it instead of the Wii and how it was going to make me money. There were a lot of emails about how you can make money online. All you needed was time and a computer. I had a computer now but didn't stop to think that whatever time I had was taken up with sleep. I tried everything. There was an email that said a woman from Provincetown got rich working from home in only four hours a week. They even had her picture. *They had a picture, it had to be real, right?* It never occurred to me that there are only about five people living in Provincetown and I pretty much knew all of them. After a bit of research, I surmised this woman was a fake and gave up on that company. But first I called them to question the existence of said person and they didn't deny using fake people to get computer users to sign up. I demanded they return my $3.79 shipping fee for the completely free kit.

I started taking surveys online for pay. And I did get paid too, it wasn't a scam. I got paid a whopping six cents per hour, approximately. I took surveys on banking, fast food, frozen food, pet food, gluten free food, politics, commercials, magazines, medicine, laundry detergent, menstrual products, toilet paper, toothpaste, you name it. If there was a survey out there that I qualified for, I took it. The companies tell you they are legitimate and you can earn hundreds by doing their surveys. What they don't tell you is that it will take you hundreds of years to earn any real money and sometimes you must be willing to spend a little money to earn most of the hundreds they promise. I wasn't. I was trying to save, after all. So I signed up for sweepstakes instead, including Publishers Clearing House.

Zack had gotten me into filling out the forms and mailing them back because who knew, someone had to win, right? But now that I had a computer I could do them all the time without paying the postage fees. And I did. And every month I would get an email saying someone from Eastham with the initials YD would win. It must have been legitimate because they had the name of my local florist and TV station in the mailing. But then nothing. Eastham wasn't very big either; who were all these other people from Eastham with my initials that were winning? How come I wasn't hearing about it? Yet every day I turned on my computer with the expectation that I would somehow be rich and could stay home and sleep.

When the surveys and sweepstakes didn't pan out, I read another email about how I could become a Mystery Shopper in my spare time and instantly get paid to go out to eat, to shop, and to go to the movies. I signed up and waited. And waited. And waited. Two months later I received a call from a gentleman who needed me to complete an assignment. I would have been suspicious that his voicemail didn't identify an actual company but his message signed off with "God Bless," so how bad could he be?

We set up the covert mission. I was to go to a vacuum cleaner store to find out what type of bags they were selling for a $1,500 vacuum cleaner. I needed to look like I was someone who would own a $1,500 vacuum cleaner. I didn't. My wardrobe was not that of a woman who would own a $1,500 vacuum. On a good day it was Dress Barn and Lane Bryant. Often Dr. T would give us girls in the front gift cards to Talbots so we could look spiffy at the reception desk. I could wear one of those Talbots outfits, but my Payless shoes would give me away. And even if I could borrow a Gucci bag, Prada shoes, and a Neiman Marcus ensemble, my tripping in the Prada shoes and pulling up in my dented, 2005 Corolla with the chipped paint job wasn't going to back up my story. Plus, what I knew of vacuum cleaners was nil. Sometimes I had trouble turning them on.

Twenty years before, when I had moved into my first single girl apartment, I borrowed Laurie's vacuum and couldn't figure out how to work it. I called but she was in the shower. Drew was four and answered the phone.

Me: "Good morning, Drew, is your mother there?"

Drew: "She's in the shower."

Me: "Oh, I had a question for her. I can't figure out how to turn on this stupid vacuum, you don't know how, do you?"

Drew: "Auntie, you see the tall part? The part with the hose? There is a black button on it. You push that."

Me: "Oh, I see it now. Wow, I can't believe I missed that. Thanks, kid."

I pushed the button. It didn't work.

Me: "I don't think that's it Drewbie, it didn't turn on."

Drew: "You push the button UP Auntie!"

Me: "Oh …"

With the whir of the vacuum motor he hung up and went back to "Barney" or "Lamb Chop," or whatever crazy kid's show made him smarter than his college-educated yet technically inept aunt.

So how was I to pull off this mission? I needed a plan, a cover story. I came up with one. I created a fictitious boyfriend named Bob. Bob and I had a terrible problem. I couldn't afford a $1,500 vacuum cleaner but Bob's wealthy parents could. We had been using their retirement home in the Cape all winter as a secluded love nest on the weekends and now they were retiring for good after traveling in Europe all winter. I needed to clean the place up as best I could, fast. Did I mention that my fake boyfriend Bob and I also had two fake dogs that were not supposed to be in the house? So I needed to use their fancy vacuum cleaner and get lots of bags to replace what they had so they wouldn't know how much cleaning we needed to do.

Pretty brilliant, I thought. But the store clerk wasn't interested. When he learned I only wanted to buy bags and not an actual $1,500 vacuum, he tried to rush me out of the store as quickly and rudely as possible. That annoyed me. I had worked the Cape tourist scene and believed visitors deserved the best. If we wanted their money, they should get us at our friendliest, most helpful selves. I played more vacuum dumb than I had to, even making the salesman demonstrate how to replace the bags with a similar model in the store display. It was fun. I felt like Tom Cruise in *Mission Impossible*. I felt I took a stand for customers everywhere who should be treated with respect, even if they only wanted vacuum cleaner bags. $1,500 vacuum cleaner owners unite!

I turned in my report detailing how they only sold the generic brand of bags and waited suspiciously for my thirty dollar payment. How could it be that easy? It had to be a fraud. At least I didn't have much to lose except my precious time. But the payment did come. And the check cleared. Perhaps this could be my second career that would help with the medical bills and to cushion a safety net in my savings account.

My next assignment came several months later. It was for a different company and it involved counting heads at a movie theater. It was not a mystery shop. I even had a letter from Warner Bros to the theater manager detailing what I was doing, not to charge me, and as long as I didn't annoy them too much, they were not to kick me out. Generally I am not an annoying person, so I wasn't kicked out. Most of the theater staff seemed to be in their early twenties and thought a letter from Warner Bros was cool. We bonded. The movie and I, however, did not. The movie I was to count heads for was *Inception*, starring Leonardo DiCaprio. I was excited. Everyone was waiting for this movie to come out and early reviews gave it the highest praise possible. I could see the movie for free twenty times over two weekends as long as I counted the heads in attendance with me.

Spoiler Alert! No disrespect intended to Mr. DiCaprio or Warner Bros but I thought the movie sucked. And furthermore, it is not, I repeat, NOT for people with multiple sclerosis or people with any type of cognitive issues whatsoever. It was about a guy who could manipulate dreams for profit. But he had to be in your dream to do it. And his dreams could take over your dreams. Or, your subconscious dreams could take over your current dream. Or his subconscious dreams could take over your subconscious dreams. Or, someone else could invade the dream and their dream could take over all the other dreams. You never knew whose dream was whose and if it was in the past or the present or the future.

For someone who has trouble processing information on all but the most basic level even before my diagnosis, I was completely lost. The frugal me insisted on getting the most out of this job by seeing every free movie I could. Thus, I struggled through the first viewing of the whole film, but barely. It was certainly loud enough to keep me awake as the pounding in my head was off the charts. Truly, if the neighborhood could hear the pounding in my head in conjunction with the craziness of the movie volume, the theater would have been fined for noise violations. I didn't have to watch the whole movie every showing but I did have to watch the first twenty minutes to make sure everyone who came in late or left for popcorn was properly documented. So I could quote the first twenty minutes of movie dialogue but still couldn't tell you what the heck was going on.

During an evening showing, six teenagers showed up thirty minutes late and were furious that the movie didn't start at a time convenient for them. The manager was happy to sell them tickets, but so there were no complaints, he stated that they had missed a significant portion of the story. They left, and in talking to him about it afterwards he mentioned how he didn't want them mad at him if they were totally confused. "They would have no idea what was going on since the beginning is actually the end," he said.

"Huh???" I asked.

Him: "You know, you saw it. The way the movie starts is actually the end of the movie."

Me: "Oh yeah, of course. We wouldn't want them to be confused by that."

On a late showing of the feature a dad and his 19-year-old son were willingly and excitedly waiting in line to see it for a second time. The son was talking about how thrilled he was that Warner Bros didn't mess with the director's vision, and how the film spoke to him on so many levels and dimensions, and how it was an amazing piece of art. Much to my shock, the dad agreed. And when he could tell that I didn't, he kindly pointed out that it was really a movie one had to see two or three times to completely grasp. I barely survived watching it once. Yet one by one theater goers were leaving the auditorium in complete awe.

Several days later my mom and I had dinner with Christine and Bill, friends of ours who had just seen *Inception*. They too were in awe. They pointed out how they couldn't wait to see it again and how it wasn't until the movie was over that they figured out that the old guy in the beginning was really DiCaprio.

"What?" I asked. "No way. The old guy was the Asian guy."

"No," they told me. "The old guy was DiCaprio."

"But the old guy was Asian. DiCaprio is not Asian."

"But it was his dream," they replied.

Again, my advice is if you have MS and are dealing with cognitive issues this is not the movie for you. Try something light and easy to follow. I think *Toy Story 3* was out at the same time. That is one I probably should have tried to sneak into. I might have understood it better.

Since I needed to count every showing of the particular dates, I spent two weekends in the theater, leaving only to sleep at night and trying to sleep in the lobby after twenty minutes of each show. I lived on buttered popcorn, M&M's, Junior Mints, and diet Coke, pretty much consuming the Warner Bros paycheck I received two months later. It became clear that mystery shopping was perhaps not the best solution to my money and health woes.

CONGRATULATIONS

It wasn't just my body aching weird aches or my head shouting bizarre shouts that was throwing me off. After the diagnosis, people were saying unusual things. Two months after I received my news, a kind woman from my small town was very happy to bump into me in the grocery store. She ran over and gave me a big, bear hug. As she was doing so she exclaimed, "Congratulations! I am so happy for you!" She began asking me if I was wild with excitement, if my family was thrilled beyond belief, and would I please put her down for the prime rib, she would send in her RSVP as soon as she got the invite. It might have been me, but that response seemed a little odd.

"Excuse me Angela, but I have no idea what you're talking about."

"I heard the news," she said, smiling, "you know, the news about you getting married."

She seemed in shock that I was in shock.

"I'm not getting married, at least not that I know of. Why, who did you hear I was marrying? Maybe I am and I don't know it." *If it's somebody good, maybe I will go for it.*

Her look of shock turned to horror. I surmised that someone else native to our small town was engaged, and Angela heard about her in the same bit of chitchat where she heard about my latest medical news.

It seemed the best explanation as that tended to be how small town gossip worked.

She apologized profusely, but I was still curious about whom she had heard I was marrying. Maybe my crush had a crush on me too, and mentioned it to someone we knew in common (not totally out of the question in a small town). Now a wedding was being planned and everyone simply forgot to tell me. Maybe my mom was dress shopping as we spoke and my dad, in great relief, was making deals on a reasonable reception venue. Maybe my baby sis Suzanne, our own family event planner, had already started selecting menus. Had my sister Audrey looked at flights so she and her family could come up from Florida? I stared off at the cereal aisle dreamily considering what music would be best. Was Keith Richards singing "You've Got the Silver" too edgy for a wedding? Would the groom and his family like it? Then I thought maybe Zack was back and was going to surprise me, and our whole town was in on it.

Funny how, like a nine-year-old little girl, I was content to stage my wedding with either a recent crush or my prior soul mate. As I made wedding plans in my mind, Angela began to back away, embarrassed. I came to my senses. These fantasies were fun explanations for the mixup but the likely story was in the confused gossip details. I didn't correct her. I didn't want to make her feel worse for something that only offended me if she had heard I was marrying somebody great when I really wasn't. Maybe she heard I was marrying somebody awful and then she should be relieved with my actual news of having a disease. I could assume, however, that if she heard I was marrying a jerk she wouldn't have been so delighted. But she didn't name my anonymous groom so I would never know. She headed off toward produce and since produce was where the veggies lived I, of course, went in another direction.

Angela and I never actually discussed the multiple sclerosis diagnosis and when I would see her later, we would say hello, how are you, how is your summer going, the normal stuff you say when you meet someone in the grocery store. Congratulations might not have been an actual reaction to my bummer news but the timing of it sure made me wonder for a bit. Most people reacted more normally, saying things like: *What? No Way! What did you say? You have multiple sclerosis? I'm so sorry. Oh no … Man, that sucks!*

The opposite end of the reaction spectrum was the not-so-sympathetic feedback I received from my boss, Dr. T. Five months after being diagnosed, I called in sick one day. This was the only day I had called in sick in over a year at least, and, considering the state of my health, I didn't feel it was unreasonable. At that point I had often come to work exhausted, terrified, achy, and before the steroids, barely able to walk. I worked through it all, even working overtime while Jackie took a ten-day vacation six weeks after the news. I was managing, but this one day the aches were too great, the rattling in my brain too extreme, and the fatigue so bad that I didn't have the energy to get out of bed. So I called in sick, not expecting a problem since Jackie was in and the schedule wasn't that bad.

I guess Jackie appreciated my role in the office more than I had realized. When she heard I wouldn't be in, she broke down and told everyone in the office how horribly unfair it was that she had to work alone because I was sick. When I came in the next day, I was in the middle of trying to catch up on the great mountain of work that had been piled on my desk when Dr. T said to me, "Watching you go through this is very stressful to my office." What was I supposed to say to that? *Ummm, I'm sorry. I hope they find a cure for MS so your employees won't be too stressed about my health problems.* That's what I wanted to say, but I didn't. I shrugged and did what I always did. I continued sorting through the piles, one exhausting task at a time.

Don't get me wrong, most people expressed legitimate concern and asked if there was anything they could do, the normal comments that make you grateful for the people in your life. And there were other responses that made me laugh and helped me understand that I wasn't alone. My friend Samantha also lived in Florida during this time, and after I told her everything and described the shots I would have to do, I received this text message from her:

"wish I was wu 2 support u n look away n cringe while u do shot."

The jury was still out on whether the craziness was my own, but the reactions from Angela in the store and from Dr. T seemed to me so extreme that I just had to analyze them. I asked Laurie about the weirdest reaction she had received to news of her diagnosis.

"An elderly, kind of eccentric lady I hadn't seen in a while just said, 'Oh, damn!' when I told her I had MS."

We both laughed. "Oh, damn!" seemed like a perfect response.

We let our brains ramble about this a bit. I had wished I had a perfect response to Dr. T's comment. I had been reading a lot about other people with multiple sclerosis, and Laurie had years of experience. We started brainstorming good and bad responses to the news, and which reactions deserved a harsh comeback.

We had so much fun tossing remarks back and forth, it became therapeutic. Then we thought maybe it could be helpful to others as well. Perhaps we could publish our thoughts to tell people what not to say to someone who has MS and to give MSers a quick answer at the ready if they need one. Thus we created our list of the top ten things to never say to someone with multiple sclerosis:

10. Smug person: "Are you sure it's not just all in your head?"

> **MSer**: "Of course it is all in my head! And a bit in my c-spine too. Sit down. Let me show you my MRI."

9. Shallow person: "That's not MS. That's old age."

> **MSer**: "So for some strange reason I have just aged thirty years in five seconds. I feel so much better now."

8. Helpful person: "You should look into (insert list of wildly bizarre alternative remedies here)."

> **MSer**: "Thing is, I am a little overwhelmed right now and that is about the tenth suggestion I have received just in the last hour on things to look into that might or might not be helpful. How about you look into it and get back to me, okay? Great, thanks."

7. Clueless person: "Oh, that's nothing. I get that all the time."

MSer: "Really? Nothing? Damn, I have been shooting my-self up with drugs made from Chinese hamster ovary cells for the fun of it. Think I am making that up? Get a magnifying glass and check out a box of interferon injections."

6. Conceited, self-centered person: "You're tired? I'm really tired, too."

MSer: "Tired huh? Last night I started sobbing at the idea of brushing my teeth as my arm was too exhausted to lift the tube of toothpaste. Are you THAT tired?"

5. Ignorant person: "You could die from this, you know?"

MSer: "Dammit it! I thought this meant I was going to live forever. Geez!"

4. Optimistic person: "But you don't look sick to me."

MSer: "That's wonderful news. Could you call my doctor and let her know? Maybe she got it all wrong."

3. Sarcastic person: "You can't just blame MS for every thing."

MSer: "Watch me!"

2. Curious person: "Isn't that what Michael J. Fox has?"

MSer: "No, this is the disease that Montel Williams has. You know, the disease where he wrote that book and said it was OK to smoke pot. Got any on you?"

1. Opportunistic person: "How do you get one of those handicapped parking thingies anyway?"

MSer: "You've got to go see my buddy Vinnie down at the RMV. He hands them out for fifty dollars and a subscription to the beer of the month club. Here, let me give you his number."

Laurie and I were really just blowing off MS steam. The last remark seemed a little too familiar as Christopher had been ready to drive me to the RMV on the day of the diagnosis. He was trying to cheer me up, wasn't he?

Eventually, we agreed that most people were kind and who could blame them if they said such absurd things—everything about MS was absurd. We decided that if anyone asked us what an appropriate thing to say to someone who had been recently diagnosed was, we would tell them that swearing was the best way to go. "Oh, damn!" seemed fabulous to us.

WALKING ACROSS THE BAY ON A SUNNY DAY

Here is what I was thinking as I walked across Cape Cod Bay to Plymouth one summer day six months after my diagnosis:

1. What in the hell have I just done?

2. Is it real? Can I really wake up on Monday and not have to go to the office? Can I really just stay in and rest?

3. How on earth am I going to pay my bills?

4. When people ask me what I do for a living, what will I say?

5. What in the hell have I just done?

Why list the last one twice? Probably because I was thinking it double time. Perhaps I should back up. It was 11:35 a.m. on a sunny, beautiful Friday in June. I had started out wearing my mother's shorts, shirt, and shoes. But as the shoes were too big for me, I had ditched them by a bench that sat between the parking lot and the beach.

I wasn't supposed to be on the beach. I was supposed to be back at the office, banging my head against my desk, while a lady named Evelyn tried to teach me the very basics of our new computer system. A new computer system that was supposed to solve all of our problems, problems I didn't know we had, once we'd mastered its convoluted, multilayered, multicolored operating system. All around me, my coworkers, who had achieved the basic knowledge, were eager to move on. To kill time while I tried to catch up and recapture what I had learned during the previous four days, they talked about late-spring barbecues and the manicures they needed to have done before the barbecue but after they made the potato salad. I could hear all their chatter in my left ear, while the trainer drilled on in my right ear. Meanwhile, Dr. T would interrupt to ask her questions on issues so far in advance of where we were supposed to be, that often she didn't bother to answer him. And this was the day we were supposed to be completely trained and ready to be on our own. When Dr. T wasn't asking our trainer questions, he was seeing patients, and I was supposed to know what to do with them when he was done. I didn't. At this point, I was so mixed up I barely knew my name.

Through all of this, the phones were ringing and, as my colleagues were very busy (barbecues being important during that time of year), I was answering them and didn't have a clue what to do with the calls. This was new for me. I had been the person in the office who always knew what to do with calls when they came in, the one everyone else came to ask what to do with calls, even, and especially, Dr. T.

I had always been the point person of the front desk. I knew my job and did it well. But in the six months since the news, with the exhaustion continuing every day, I had noticed I was starting to make more mistakes. Little mistakes really, the ones we all made. But I was making them more often than I ever had. I had always been the one who fixed mistakes, so I was catching them before they blew up and felt I could keep things basically under control. But I was worried about the system change.

Computers and I weren't best friends anyway. The computer revolution had come to our small school when I was a sophomore, and I missed it. My beloved librarian became so excited about the new computer that it became her focus. I felt I had to take a stand for the books and ignored it. When computer classes became mandatory in senior year, I took them but only because I had to. I went off to college with a typewriter and felt I was on track. Entering the working world four years later, I realized computers were here to stay and learned only what I needed to perform my job, whichever job it might have been at the time. Including this job at Dr. T's that I had held successfully for over seven years.

On Monday, day one of the training, I left work feeling that the new computer system was complex but I could handle it. *So the next week will be tough, so what. It happens. But things will get figured out,* I reasoned.

By Tuesday, day two, I had no recollection of what I'd learned on Monday. It was all a crazy mash of information that was impossible to sort. The complexities of the system were beyond me. Close this window without saving or you'll throw your data out of sync. Save this screen or you'll lose everything. To get to screen D, you must exit A, open and save B, bypass C and then minimize B to open D. Everything was color coordinated. Basic blue meant a patient was late. Light blue meant the patient was early. Dark blue meant the patient had checked in. Aquamarine meant the patient had a balance. Turquoise meant the patient had a credit. Sky blue meant the patient had insurance. On and on it went. Each room in the office also had a different shade of a color. And the different types of appointments had different shades of color as well. To get to the chart to show what colors meant what, you had to repeat the process of exiting A, saving B, etc. The system that was going to make all of our jobs so much easier now required ten steps to book an appointment when the old system required only three. I couldn't even remember the steps you had to take to get to the screen to figure out the steps you needed to take to book an appointment. And I needed one of those 64-color boxes of crayons to sort out all the colors.

I had been writing everything down on paper so I could go back later and enter data correctly when I knew the system. The piles of paper were growing. My overwhelmed senses were starting to affect my vision. There were spots out of the corner of my eyes making the colorful computer screen just a blurry mess. And it was all making me dizzy. I went home frustrated and, in tears, went to bed.

On Wednesday, day three, I went in determined to figure this out. We hadn't even covered the basics and we only had two more days before we would start seeing patients and be expected to have this all down. It got better throughout the day and I was starting to feel more confident. Then the system crashed. Dr. T was golfing. My coworkers had already left for the day. It was just me and Evelyn, and the incoming phone calls, and my growing piles of papers and promises to call back when the training was over. At one point, I called Dr. T. and expressed my growing concern. He told me it would all be fine, not to worry and to call the computer techs and tell them Dr. T said to come over right away and to make sure they fixed everything.

On Thursday, I was completely lost again. I sat Dr. T down and told him I was really in trouble. He said I wasn't, I would be fine. Then he offered to lessen my burden and told me he would make sure my coworkers answered the phone so I didn't have to be interrupted when I was trying to grasp all of this new technology. I explained how the most difficult thing was processing and remembering all the information and that I feared MS was affecting my concentration. He told me it wasn't, he was a doctor and he should know. He said it was hard for all of us and don't worry, he'd help. He then asked the only new employee to take care of phone calls and if she had any questions, to just ask one of the girls up front. She chose to ask me.

Only minutes later, Dr. T received a call from a colleague. The colleague informed Dr. T that a mutual patient had been treated rudely when she had called our office. Dr. T came out front and interrupted training, demanding to know who on his staff took the call. The one thing I knew that week was that I hadn't talked to this particular patient. When no one admitted being responsible, he instructed me to immediately stop what I was doing and learning, and teach the entire office how to answer the phone, a job they had all been doing for years. Still, that night I stayed late with trainer lady. We were live the next day and hadn't covered anything but the most basic information. And I knew I didn't know it. But when I left that night I felt better. I was trying, knowledge would come. It had to. It always had before.

On Friday, the first patient checkout was a mess. Computer training lady showed us where the mistakes were. My coworkers got the information and understood what went wrong. I didn't. She pointed out that I had taken notes on the information. I looked at them and they were not in any language I recognized. It was my handwriting and so they must have been my notes. But I had absolutely no comprehension of what the words on the page meant, the thought I had when I was writing them and what to do with them, even if I had written them. We had four more hours of training and over 85 percent of my workload still to cover and I didn't understand the 15 percent we already had. I had no idea how to handle the stack of callbacks and assignments noted on my growing slips of paper.

I suddenly realized I had no idea how to do my job. The job I had held for over seven years was now even more foreign to me than when I started. The one thing I felt I still knew how to do was file charts, which was moot as they were about to be stored digitally—the point of this new system was to go paperless. I was the one who knew everything there was to know about the front desk, and it was gone. The realization of that almost made me collapse in Dr. T's private office. I was able to steady myself, but barely. I told him I had to leave, to quit, I had no choice. He told me to stay, I would be fine, I was just nervous, it was new to all of us. But I knew that wasn't it. Perhaps he was trying to be sympathetic, but in reality, the situation would continue: he would promise help, say it would all be fine, and then dump something else in my lap for me to handle. That was our employer/employee dynamic; it had been this way for years and usually worked, with or without added stress. But now I had absolutely no idea how to handle anything, nor any clue or ability to learn how to handle everything. MS was seriously messing with my brain as much as it was messing with my body and there was no end in my blurry sight. I understood that no matter what he said, Dr. T and my coworkers didn't understand and would never accept my difficulties. It was my disease, it was my problem and would remain my problem while I was still expected to excel at my job with little support. I grabbed my purse and walked out, telling my coworkers I needed to leave. They were in shock. I was the rock. I didn't leave. Who was going to cover for them when they left early to get ready for their weekend barbecues?

I made it to my car and stood in the beautiful day while I tried to breathe and gather myself for the drive away from the office. I tried to think about what walking out actually meant. If I left, I might never be able to return. But my head hurt so much from thinking and trying to learn that I knew I couldn't go back in. I had to get out of there, out of the parking lot and away from the office. Driving away was a terrifying step away from the security I'd known, and I didn't exactly know what I'd be driving *to*. It physically hurt to think but I couldn't stop thinking. It's funny how small things come to your mind as you make big decisions. As I started my car I realized I had left string cheese unconsumed in my desk. It would stink up the office. That was gross. It would seem like I had done it on purpose. Do I go back and get it after all of this? How weird would that be? Do I text Terry and tell her about it so she can throw it away? But Terry may be mad at me and would she welcome me giving her this strange task in light of the craziness that was my quitting? I spent ten minutes in the office lot analyzing what to do about string cheese before I finally drove away.

I stopped at a rest area and called my mom. We chatted aimlessly for about five minutes when she realized we shouldn't be aimlessly chatting, I should be at work.

"What's going on, anyway? Why are you calling me at 11:00 on a Friday? Aren't you at work?"

"I think I just quit. No, I did. I just quit. I guess. I'm not sure."

"Where are you?"

"I just pulled over on Route 6. I left string cheese in my desk. I don't know if I should go back and get it."

"Can you drive?"

"Of course I can drive. I have been driving since high school. Don't you remember when I dented your car?" *Geez, sometimes my mom wasn't that smart.*

"I meant, are you driving safely even though you must be so upset?"

"Umm sure, I think so."

My ever-practical mother sensed my hysteria and suggested that I stop worrying about string cheese and come to her house.

I did. I fell onto her leather recliner and told her the story. As I replayed it back for her, it became clearer. I had just quit my job. I don't do that, ever. I have left jobs when the time was right, with proper notice and with time to train a replacement, but I have never just walked out. But I had never lost all knowledge of how to do my job either. How could I not quit? I had learned stuff and then completely forgotten it, and the reminder lessons weren't working. My coworkers understood everything, but I had no clue. I thought of the big tumor-looking mass in my brain as my head was throbbing.

Questions upon questions were zooming in and out of my thoughts. I couldn't think, but I also couldn't stop thinking.

My mom said I was going to make myself crazy. It sounded to her like I quit and that was likely a good thing. The tensions at work were not helping the stress of dealing with an illness. She said what I needed now was to breathe. "Don't worry about the questions, we'll figure them out later. I'll help. Right now, you need to go for a walk. The tide is low, let's go walk the flats."

"I can't go for a walk now!" I said, "I just quit my job! Plus, I'm in work clothes, from Talbots no less. You can't walk the flats in clothes from Talbots unless you are modeling for their catalog where no one ever gets muddy."

"You can borrow some of my things." My mom gave me comfy black shorts and a bright pink top that she never got back. I slid into her sandals, which were three sizes too big, and shuffled and flopped over the gravel driveway to her car. I took them off when we hit the beach. We started on the flats and after a bit she turned to head back to the car but told me to take my time. The water was beautiful, and the pleasant splashing sound my feet made in the tide pools helped soothe my headache. I kept walking and as I did so, the stress started to ease.

I was really done! The piles and piles of callbacks on my desk were not my problem anymore. The perfect day seemed like an omen. I had tried, given it my all. But some things were out of my control. This week's mounting stresses were my brain and body's way of telling me things needed to change. It was time for something new. The headache melted into relief. MS or no MS, I was smart and strong. I would handle whatever came my way.

I walked until the water of Cape Cod Bay reached my thighs. I had no idea how far out I was, but I knew if it wasn't low tide it would have been over my head and I would have been swimming for a while. No one else was around me and it was time to head back.

Back in the car, my mom said she was just starting to get worried when she saw me again. I had gone so far out that even on this completely clear day she had trouble seeing her bright pink shirt.

We went to lunch, where I was shuffling again in her sandals. The questions in my head returned, but slightly more peacefully, and with my mom's promises of help if needed, alternated between curious and only mildly panicked. I wondered if Dr. T would be willing to pay me for my unused vacation time? Where would I get my reading suggestions from if not from the patients? How do I figure out if I can qualify for Cobra, MS being an incredibly expensive disease? When people asked what I did for a living, what would I tell them? How much would they take out in taxes if I cashed in my IRA? What should I tell patients when I bumped into them around town? And, most importantly, what do I do about that damn string cheese?

THE
LITTLE THINGS

After lunch, outside of the air-conditioned restaurant and away from the bay breeze, it was hot. My mom said I should go home and rest, but I felt I should go home and sort this mess out. My brain and body were tumbling through a bizarre mix of peace and panic. I was thirsty and craving my favorite thirst quencher, a fountain Diet Coke with a ton of ice. Water alone doesn't do it for me. Diet Coke in a can or bottle doesn't do it either. Something about that particular brand of soda in a frosty cold plastic cup filled with ice was what worked for me.

I stopped at a convenience store and then sat in my car panicking. Fountain drinks here cost eighty-three cents. I didn't have a job. I had absolutely no business wasting eighty-three cents at this point in my life. I needed to save, to be cautious and thrifty. There was nothing wrong with tap water from my kitchen sink, even if it was from a well and turned my bathtub blue. Now that I wasn't working I would just have to get used to it, even if it turned my insides blue. Maybe blue would make the lesions in my brain and on my spine more colorful, freak the MRI techs out. That would at least be fun. And I probably even had ice somewhere in my freezer. Maybe the same ice that had been there since last summer, but I couldn't be particular now. No, I wasn't going to foolishly spend money, no Diet Coke for me.

But I wanted it, dammit. I had had a stressful day. Didn't I deserve a treat? And wouldn't Diet Coke help me calm down and sort out my life? I walked in, filled the plastic cup with a ton of ice and the cherished beverage and defiantly pulled out a dollar bill at the counter. I took some comfort in the fact that at least I would get change back. No putting the two pennies in the need a penny take a penny tray—I needed to save everything.

The clerk behind the register seemed busy with paperwork and barely looked up as he said, "You're all set." I laughed, figuring he was joking. But he didn't move. I slid my dollar across the counter.

"There's no charge today," he said.

"What? How can that be?" I guessed he was a wise guy and continued to thrust one of my seemingly last dollars at him.

"It's free," he insisted, sliding my dollar back in my direction. "It's Friday, a no-charge-fountain-beverage Friday."

"Really?" I was shocked. Was it true? I could quench my thirst AND save my eighty-three cents?

I began to thank him profusely and tell him how much I loved the store, how I only shopped there and it was because of excellent customer service like his. What a wonderful company to offer a treat like this one. I told him how kind of them it was and how I would remember it always and continue to only shop there from now on.

"I am in your debt, and I am so grateful. I will tell all my friends how great your store is and make sure they all shop here too!"

He seemed to be slowly backing away from the counter. I realized that a line had formed and in declaring my appreciation, I was keeping other customers from getting their free Friday fountain beverage, not to mention, sort of freaking everyone out. I headed to my car with my dollar still in my pocket and a big grin on my face. I no longer had a job, but I had a free soda. I was going to be okay. I went home, drank my soda, got into bed, and pulled a sheet over my head. Then I slept until Sunday.

HIDING WITH MY DUCK FRIENDS

When I told Laurie what I had done, she brilliantly answered one of my major questions. I mentioned that one of the many things overwhelming me was what I should tell people when they asked what I did for a living. I had never realized how common a question that was, and how the way we answered it was so important to our identity. But Laurie was creative and she pointed out that as I had dabbled in the world of mystery shopping, I could call myself a consultant.

"But I am not doing that with any regularity. Sometimes it could be weeks and weeks before I get an assignment."

"Doesn't matter. When you do, you are consulting."

I figured that made sense. I had already drafted a formal resignation letter to Dr. T. In it, I apologized for leaving so abruptly but also tried to explain my predicament and how I felt I was no longer an asset, but a detriment to the job. I told him I had enjoyed working for him and if there was any way I could assist the staff transition by showing how I did things in the old system, I would be happy to help. Maybe I could be a consultant to Dr. T's office too.

(Later he did ask me to come in to help train the staff on my position. I went in and tried but it was useless. Everything was embedded in the new system and I wasn't able to show them anything from the old without venturing into the new. The headache came back, my former coworkers were shocked that I now knew less than they did, and I was finally able to throw away the string cheese. It had only just started to stink when I went in to make my feeble attempt at helping.)

Back to the discussion Laurie and I were having about what I should tell people I did for a living. Consulting didn't seem enough. I seemed to be decent at writing and had published some minor essays in the last few years for our local paper. "OK," Laurie said. "You're a writer. Or, if you want to get really fancy, you could say you're an artist."

"But I haven't written anything in a while."

"Doesn't matter. Go to your computer and type out 'Hello, how are you today?' and you are a writer."

I was starting to get into this. "And I volunteer a lot. Could I call myself a philanthropist?"

"Sure, why not?"

So I had answered one of my questions. I was now a consultant, a writer, and a philanthropist. All of a sudden I seemed very busy and was starting to get tired again. But it was okay. I didn't have anywhere to be at 7:45 Monday through Friday.

It felt rather decadent that first Monday morning. It was after nine when I woke up, and immediately I felt guilty. But then I realized I hadn't slept through the alarm; I just hadn't bothered to set it. *I don't have to go to work today.* I vowed to use this newfound free time wisely. I had decisions to decide, phone calls to call, and thoughts to be thought. My new job would be sorting out my life and figuring out where to go from here. And without the pressure from work, and with this new ability to get lots and lots of rest, it would be easy to sort out the next steps in my life. Problem was that it was hot, really hot.

After the beautiful Friday when I quit and seemed to walk across the bay, the weather turned into a hot, humid, cloudy one minute, sunny the next, mess. Due to an unfortunate predicament with some badly installed prefab window sills, I was not able to set up an effective window air conditioning unit in my little rented house. Friends had taken pity on me the previous summer and loaned me a portable AC that worked great, but only in one room. The room I chose was the bedroom. While I was not missing the chaos I knew was going on in the office, I was longing for the overindulgent AC there. Dr. T kept it turned so high, we all dressed in layers and sweaters during the summer months. I had always been miserable in the humidity and that was just another reason I thought I was slowly turning into an annoying old lady at the ripe age of forty. I was miserable when it was too hot and couldn't function when it was too cold. But it turns out being affected by extreme temperatures is also a symptom of MS, causing even more difficulties with thinking. Our spacey selves tend to become even spacier in the heat. Another thing I can blame on the disease. What a relief!

I moved into my bedroom for the summer. I brought in my cell phone, my $1,200 laptop, pens, notebooks, and jugs of water, as I was supposed to be keeping hydrated according to all the MS books. I got comfortable. Then I got up ten times to pee in the first two hours and took the water jugs out of my bedroom cave. I started making calls.

Question #1- How do I get COBRA insurance?

I called one office who told me to call another. That office told me they didn't know why I was told to call them and I should call the other office back. The first office then told me to call a third number. That office told me to call a particular extension, whose machine told me the lady I was trying to reach was on vacation and to call yet another number. The woman at that number finally told me what to do about COBRA, except she told me really, really fast. I was using my pillow as a desk and trying to write down what she said and I had only managed to retain "Copy your insurance card." I asked her to repeat the instructions. She did, even faster than she had the first time. The second time I retained the word "fax." I asked her again. She became aggravated and had a bit of an attitude.

"Excuse me, ma'am, the reason I can't work is that I have multiple sclerosis and it causes me to have a hard time processing information and I am slower at understanding directions. I am trying to write all this down so I get it right and won't have to bother you again. So please speak slowly so I will be able to copy what you are telling me."

She apologized and genuinely sounded sympathetic. Then she sped through the instructions again. After relaying them to me ten times, I felt I finally understood what needed to be done. But as she had annoyed me at this point with her habit of speaking faster at the more detailed parts of the instructions, I asked her to repeat them an additional two times, just to be sure I really understood. Then I took a nap.

Question #2- How much would I have to pay in taxes if I cashed in my IRA?

The next step in getting my life in order was to call my accountant. Well, I didn't actually have my own accountant. But what I did have was the super-nice lady at my local H&R Block office who had been doing my taxes for years and had been concerned when I told her of my diagnosis at February's tax meeting. She told me I would take a huge hit on my taxes if I cashed in my IRA. But what could I do? I didn't have a job.

I had some savings but had to plan for my future. The IRA had been set up through Dr. T's financial people, although it was my own account. When I got the tax information, I started calling the financial people. And calling. And leaving messages. And calling again, until I finally reached the person who could close out my IRA. And then I napped in my cool, dark bedroom cave.

Question #3- Would Dr. T be willing to pay me for my unused vacation time?

I emailed him and he asked me to meet him at his house after work later that day. He hadn't arrived when I got there, but I knew his wife and she took me on a tour of her prizewinning garden. It was still very hot and humid and getting close to dusk, so, of course, every insect in the world decided to attack me as we explored the lovely blossoms. I got descriptions of the advanced stages of landscaping that went into a prizewinning garden. I could have dealt with the bugs if I weren't the only one being pummeled. She looked fresh and beautiful, just out of the shower and dressed for dinner after a lovely day at the beach. I was sweaty, pale, and covered in greenheads and mosquitoes. When she asked me how I was doing, I could barely respond for fear of the critters flying into my mouth.

When Dr. T arrived, we went inside. He sat me down and asked me to come back and just work in the back office with him handling insurance claims only.

"It wouldn't be that hard," he insisted. "I know you say the problem is the new computer system but you would only have to learn what you need to know to handle the insurance claims and the accounting aspects of patient files. I know you don't know that now, but you could call the company and simply have them walk you through it over the phone. You would have to have them explain how to transfer the old patient files to the new system and to set up all the old employers and insurance companies in the new system as well. Then you would just handle all the claims electronically, and maybe answer the phones a bit here and there, and cover the front desk every once in a while, but that's it. Simple."

My head hurt. I was dizzy and now very itchy from a large collection of bug bites and tried not to cry as I explained how overwhelming and debilitating that all sounded. But again the words wouldn't come to my confused brain and I was rattling on and he seemed not to believe me. He wished me well and said he would sort out my vacation time and mail it to me later.

Question #4- Would I qualify for Aflac insurance?

In my cave, I pondered this and as I got ready to start those calls, I figured I needed help. I went into my spare room dripping sweat from the short ten-foot jaunt from my air-conditioned bedroom and grabbed my stuffed mama Aflac duck and baby Aflac duck. I pressed on each of their backs for "AFLAC! AFLAC! AFLACCCCCCCC!" quack inspiration as I called my insurance agent. I needed to fill out paperwork and get Dr. T to sign it. Off to the office I went for Dr. T's signature.

Jackie greeted me and told me how happy she was to see me and how she wished I hadn't left, the computer system really wasn't that hard, and she was sure I would have gotten used to it. I tried not to squirm and resisted the temptation to grab the office phone as it rang continually while she droned on and on about the new system's advantages. As she reached for the "Do Not Disturb" button on the answering machine that would send the calls directly to voice mail, I noticed that each work station had two monitors set up.

"What's with the extra screen?" I asked.

"Oh, Dr. T got those for us. With the new system there is so much information you can't see it all on one screen. Plus, you can't simply close one screen to get to another so this way we can access the different windows at one time. When you check out a patient you can go from one screen to the other and back again to read all the different windows in the patient's files at once. See, easy."

"Oh, yeah, I see that." My head immediately started pounding and then my eyes started blurring. I got the doctor's signature and got out of there as fast as possible before I wound up taking calls or fainting from looking at all the different screens too long. Realizing the messages on the machine were no longer mine to retrieve brought comfort. I wondered how long it would be before they were played.

With the paperwork mailed, I could only wait on Aflac and hope for the best. The first step in being approved for the insurance was making sure my premiums had all been paid. The pay stub on my last paycheck seemed to indicate that they were. But obviously not, as a few days later, Dr. T called to ask what to do about my "sexually transmitted disease" policy?

"WHAT?"

"I have a bill right here from Aflac requiring payment for your STD's policy."

"Dr. T, I don't have a policy on sexually transmitted diseases."

"Well, it's right here. It says your name and STD Policy."

"That can't be right," I said. "Can you mail it to me? No, better yet, I'll come up there and get it."

The stress of being in the office and the high cost of fuel were no match for my immediate need to sort out this mystery. The policy he was calling about couldn't possibly state that. I didn't even know such a thing existed. But Dr. T wouldn't make that up. Had I recently taken out a policy specifically to protect me if I came down with a sexually transmitted disease? I had been single for over a year and was way too exhausted at the end of the day to date, let alone have sex. And Aflac was designed to help people who were not able to work due to an illness. Do STDs keep you from working? I suppose they could if they were serious enough. Back up the highway I raced to collect the paperwork. And Dr. T was right, the policy did say STD. Reading the paperwork didn't solve the mystery. I headed home for another round of calls. I was pulling into my driveway when it donned on me that STD stood for *short-term disability*. Dr. T had made the assumption that STD stood for sexually transmitted diseases and my MS brain went with it, even as I was staring at the policy pamphlet that described the benefits of Short-Term Disability insurance.

I paid the final premium and waited, knowing the negative effects of my MS on my working ability would be a hard thing to prove. I could tell the insurance people the things that were going on in my head as I was faltering at work but it was entirely up to them to choose to believe me or not. Especially since what was affecting me was my cognition and difficulty in learning the new computer system. Would they pay on such a thing? I had paperwork from both doctors stating the problem but I knew it was a long shot. I cuddled and squeezed my Aflac ducks for support. My Aflac agent called. My policy would likely be denied because it looked as if my beloved physician's assistant had forged my doctor's signature. I looked at the paperwork and saw that the signatures were similar, but that didn't seem like something Mandy would do. Ever. The agent said I needed to get Dr. N to re-sign it. I called the office. Dr. N was on a six-month leave and out of the country. She would not be able to sign anything until late fall. I called the Aflac agent back.

"Maybe another doctor could sign for her. You might need to do a whole new exam but it's worth a try. It's really your only shot."

I called the office again and was told the covering doctor was in but only for another half hour. If I wanted to talk to her, I'd better hurry. I rushed out the door, pausing only to squeeze my ducks once more for luck, and got to the office in ten minutes. The covering doctor had already left. I explained my plight to her receptionist. She looked at the paperwork.

"But this IS Dr. N's signature. Mandy didn't sign for her. See how the N's and M's in both names are different? They do look alike but are not the same. I know the covering doctor won't sign this as Dr. N already has."

I went home and called my agent.

"I don't know. The company may not believe that they are not the same. You might be denied." Squeeze, squeeze, squeeze went my ducks. Only in an ironic MS world would I be denied short-term disability insurance based on a false belief that a doctor's signature was forged, as opposed to being denied because my symptoms were hard to prove.

But I wasn't denied. Aflac came through and my ducks and I rested peacefully for the next few weeks.

VITAMIN D IS NOT CLASS D

Here is another strange thing about multiple sclerosis, in case anyone wants to start a list. The sun can *prevent* MS, but if you *have* MS, the sun can hurt you. Research shows that people who live near the equator, where they get more sun daily than anyone else on the planet, have fewer instances of the illness. But if you have MS, it is best to stay out of the heat the sun radiates.

The reason seems to be that, along with all the dangerous ultraviolet rays that the sun emits, it also helps our bodies make our own vitamin D. Vitamin D seems to be good at preventing and helping fight MS. Perhaps the more vitamin D you obtain, the less likely it is that you will get MS. The jury is still out on this. No one really knows anything except that if you move to the equator, you are less likely to contract MS. (Note: your risk of contracting the West Nile virus, yellow fever, and various types of cancers increases. Your choice.)

Once you have MS, the heat from the sun can intensify all your MS symptoms. However, if you are able to withstand the heat, it is good to get a little natural vitamin D. But too much sun can lead to skin cancer risks. Wear sunscreen, but not too much. Get out in the sun, but only for a short time. What's an MS sufferer to do?

In my little New England town, with its variety of seasons and temperatures, I went to the beach often. I found gazing at the water comforting. But I was as likely to go to the beach on a rainy, cold winter's day as I was on a 90-degree day in August. Dr. M discovered I was extremely deficient in vitamin D. I took this as a failure. Poor eating habits aside, I did drink milk and eat yogurt often, and weren't those good sources of the precious nutrient? Seems not enough. Dr. M promptly put me on a prescription source of vitamin D: 55,000 IUs. I did not know what an IU was, but 55,000 of it seemed like a lot. Later, I learned that IU stood for international units and was even more convinced that was a lot. I couldn't picture 55,000 of anything. 55,000 pieces of confetti thrown on New Year's Eve in New York City? 55,000 blades of grass in the local football field and baseball field combined? 55,000 pieces of rainbow sprinkles in the massive sprinkle canister at the local ice cream shop? *No,* I thought, *stop thinking about unhealthy foods.* 55,000 seeds on the outside of strawberries at the local organic strawberry farm? It was hard to picture. Dr. M wanted me on one of these tablets every day for seven days and then once a week after that.

She called in the prescription, and three days later I headed to my local pharmacy to pick it up (apparently I wasn't in that much of a hurry—maybe the sun's rays were slowing me down). My pharmacist thought 55,000 was a lot too.

"We haven't filled that Rx yet," he said. "That is an awful lot of vitamin D and it doesn't seem right."

"Have you talked to my doctor?" I asked.

"Oh, we put the Rx to the side. We are waiting to talk to her."

I asked, "Well, have you called her? What happens next?"

He gave me a blank look. Perhaps he thought Dr. M was psychic and would know there was a problem and call them. I went home and left her office a message.

Two days later the pharmacist called. "I have heard from your doctor and it seems that is right. She does want you to take that much. But that is an awful lot and I am not comfortable with giving it to you all at once. I will fill the Rx for three days and then you will have to come back to get the rest."

He seemed to be saying this almost accusingly. Did he think Dr. M and I were in some type of cahoots over the vitamin D? Did he suspect we had an evil plan to dole it out to unsuspecting folks who were already drinking their fair share in their milk?

I picked up the stuff and took it for three days. On the second day I went back for the rest. But no, I had to come back on the third day to get part two. Did the pharmacist confuse vitamin D with class D? Did he think I was going to sell it? Maybe he was on to something. This was the same pharmacist who filled my legal speed scrip without batting an eye, but for a whole lot of vitamins, he was holding back? Maybe I should try to make some money on this. "Yeah, try this stuff, I don't know why but my pharmacist refuses to give me more than a little at a time. He didn't even want to fill it all, it must be good. How much are you willing to give me?"

Of course I was not about to start selling drugs, even though the money was probably better than taking surveys online. I went back on the third day and received four more pills. When I asked about the once a week Rx, he looked at me in horror. "You'll have to come back for that after the four days are up. I told you I am not comfortable filling this all at once."

All this had happened in March and at times the sun was out. Perhaps the back and forth was designed to help me sneak in a few IUs naturally on the sunny days.

I had been on this regimen for a while when I stopped working in June. As the summer continued to be a miserable mix of sun, then clouds, then rain, then sun again amidst rotten humidity, I continued to be a mess. The thought of heading outside to get my vitamin D naturally was out of the question. I stayed locked in my bedroom cave with the AC blasting, taking my sun in a bottle and drinking milk. Well, let's be honest. It was summer and hot so I was probably getting my milk in the form of ice cream and who knew how many vitamins were in that. I ventured out of my house only when I had to because I was usually exhausted just walking to the car. The heat was miserable but I did my best.

When I did venture out I noticed that my car seemed to be uncomfortable too. I would be driving and it would suddenly buck forward like a nasty hiccup and be slow to get started again. I tried ignoring it, since I didn't have money for car repairs. But I had to see Dr. M in the city soon. She wanted to check my blood for my current vitamin D levels. The weather reports stated that the humidity wasn't going away any time soon. I worried about my "little engine that could" car breaking down outside of Boston. I took it to my mechanic.

Six hundred dollars drawn from my precious savings account later, my car was happy, healthy, and ready to go. The engine's computer had been faulty and was acting up. Seems my car and computers didn't get along either. I asked what caused the problem. "Sometimes the heat just gets to it," the car doctor told me. I could relate to my poor little car. Did the mechanic use my $600 to buy it six million IUs of vitamin D? Is that what made it better? I wished there was some way I could drive it into my air-conditioned bedroom cave with me to keep it from getting too fatigued. I considered slipping one of the precious vitamin D pills into the gas tank just for extra protection. I might have done it, but I was too afraid of accounting for the missing pill with my pharmacist.

But whether or not my car had MS or was nutrient deficient was answered months later. It turned out that my car was just smarter and more sensitive than other cars. The electronic control module on my vehicle was part of an upcoming recall and my car suffered first. I was able to get my money back and replenish my savings account. Feeling better, my car and I tried to patiently wait for autumn and cooler temperatures. I in my cave, and my car parked under the shadiest tree I could find, just to be safe.

THANK YOU FOR YOUR SUPPORT

In my twenties I left my little dune-shrouded hometown to work in the big city. After having spent a couple of years figuring out what I should do with my life, I landed a job working with crime victims. My professional title was Victim/Witness Advocate and I even had a fancy business card. I had been volunteering for a domestic violence shelter when I first learned of this type of work. I was thrilled to be on this career path and gave it my all. The advocate word had meaning for me; I was going to fight to save everyone! Well, at least everyone who was assigned to my busy caseload. It didn't take long to realize that there would be no saving. There was helping, guiding, meeting, listening, providing, and filing (the last two applied to information and paperwork). The core of the position was accepting that the actual saving cannot be done by someone else. In the court world

I was moving in, one could only save oneself. But it sure helped if there was someone kind and dedicated near you as you were giving it your best shot.

Although I loved the job, I loved my home more, and after eight years I decided I needed to return. Fast forward another eight years to the summer of 2010, which found me coping with my recently diagnosed multiple sclerosis. This knowledge required much pondering, but as I have previously stated, I was mostly just sleeping. One especially fatigued afternoon, my phone rang. On the line was a woman from my insurance company who was calling to assist me. It would be impolite to state here the name of the actual company so let me just say they are well known and their name includes the titles of a school and of an early settler. Let's call them Yale Colonist for the sake of this chapter. Anyway, this woman, let's call her Ada, told me she was calling from Yale Colonist and was an advocate for people with chronic illnesses. It was her job to help me through this difficult time and guide me through the insurance process. Did I have time to talk?

I could relate to this unexpected call. Hadn't I guided individuals through the scary court system during times of crisis in their lives? They usually weren't expecting my call either. I was interested in what she had to say if only in the spirit of camaraderie with my own former advocate position. Plus, I hadn't yet learned that just lying down when you are tired is not necessarily restful on its own. Talking on the phone while lying down could be exhausting, too. I lay down on my bed and got ready for a chat.

She started by asking many, many questions. Questions I had already been over with Mandy, my primary, one specialist, three MRI techs, Dr. M, and Dr. T too, for that matter. But the only other thing I had planned for the afternoon was sleeping and she said Yale Colonist really needed answers directly from me in order to better help me. Besides, hadn't I subjected crime victims to questions they had already gone over with police detectives? I responded to her questions, and as I did so, we began to bond. She then asked if my diagnosis ever made me depressed.

"Sometimes," I told her. "Mostly it is just overwhelming and I am so tired all the time that I try to sleep through the emotions."

We talked further. I told her I had been on antidepressants off and on for mood swings, but basically felt okay.

"Do you ever feel sad?"

"Sure, don't we all?"

"What do you do to handle those sad feelings?"

"Sleep."

"Do you live alone?"

"Yes."

"Do you have any weapons in your house?"

"Weapons? No, what would I do with a weapon?"

"Not even knives?"

"Knives? Oh sure, of course. Everyone has knives, but just basic steak knives."

Probably I should have figured out where she was heading. My former career required training in this same suicidal assessment. But I was sleepy. And as this call was regarding my MS diagnosis, when she talked about the knives I assumed she was leading up to my lack of coordination. Another reason vegetables were bad for me—often you have to chop them. I now had proof that there was a disease potentially exacerbating my clumsiness.

"Have you ever thought of hurting yourself?"

"What? No, not seriously anyway. I mean, no, not at all really. Once, as a kid, I had this idea to jump off the pier so that I might be able to skip school, but I didn't do it."

Have I mentioned that on top of the fatigue, cognition and the inability to focus are often real problems with my MS? Eventually I figured out what she was trying to analyze and assured her that no, I was absolutely not suicidal. I further emphasized that for the most part, I felt I was handling things well. And that, as a Catholic, I would never consider killing myself, as it would make God totally pissed off. Then I asked if we could hang up. I had just grasped the MS lesson that even talking on the phone can be tiring.

Before we said goodbye, she asked if she could continue to work with me, and she reminded me that I had agreed to let her share whatever we talked about with my doctors. She told me that Yale Colonist was very worried about me and my illness and she would like to send me some info that might be helpful. I looked to the corner of my bedroom floor where I had stacked in neat piles the information from the drug company, the information I picked up in Dr. M's office, the information the National MS Society had sent me, and the books and information I had painstakingly collected for Laurie when she was diagnosed. She had given them back to me now, and suspiciously, they looked unopened. That was rude of her not to open them. I would open them. The piles were piling up but I was going to read them all, someday.

I told advocate Ada to feel free to send me some info if she felt it would be helpful and that, sure, she could call me back in a few days to see how I was doing. I hung up and fell asleep. The next morning I received two messages. One was from one of the nurses at Dr. M's office who sounded very concerned. A fax had been sent to their office from Yale Colonist stating that I may be suicidal. Did I tell my insurance company that I was depressed and might possibly hurt myself?

"No, of course not. She completely misunderstood. I think she must have cognition issues. You should schedule her for an MRI."

The nurse did not seem to appreciate my sense of humor. I guaranteed her that I was fine and while hurting myself accidentally was likely due to my lack of coordination, I would never hurt myself intentionally. She asked some routine questions and seemed confident enough with my answers to disconnect.

The next call was from the nurse at my primary doctor's office. I had an appointment at 3:00 to get my thyroid medications refilled but they had a cancellation at 1:00; did I want to come then instead?

"Sure," I told them. When I arrived, they quickly ushered me into an exam room and Mandy was in with me in seconds.

Wow, they must be really slow today.

Mandy began our visit by reminding me why I was there and then asking me how I was doing. She was her usual friendly and compassionate self, but she seemed serious. She took her "how are you doing" questions to a deeper level and then told me she had some concerns. Seems Mandy had gotten the same fax.

"I am not going to kill myself!" I insisted.

"You know we have to check. Yale Colonist reported that you told one of their advocates you had thought about hurting your-self in the past."

"I was practically asleep! And I told her it was billions of years ago so I could skip class. You guys have made me fill out all those 'are you going to hurt yourself forms' a million times and I have always passed. I really, really am okay."

I managed to convince Mandy and she gave me my thyroid pill prescription and sent me on my way. The next week I re-ceived a huge envelope from Yale Colonist with lots of stuff to read. I added it to one of the stacks, got depressed at the ever-growing piles, and went to bed dreaming of hurting myself when the piles of paperwork and helpful information collapsed on my resting form.

When advocate Ada called me several days later and asked if I had a chance to read what she sent, I was afraid to answer. Did I admit to being a bad patient and an unappreciative insurance sub-scriber? If I told her I was too tired to read the pamphlets would she take it as a sign of my growing depression? If I lied and said I had, would she try to send me more stuff? The call became very stressful.

"I glanced through them," I replied. "I have a lot of stuff to go through and so I put them with other similar paperwork. That way, all the information I need will be together and I am going through it a little at a time."

Advocate Ada stressed how important the paperwork she sent was, and how I should read it as soon as I could. She told me that she was always available to me and to make sure I kept her num-ber in a special place in case I needed her. She asked if she could call to check in from time to time and stressed that I should call her with any questions. I thanked her and then worried. Maybe I had missed something amazing in the packet she sent me. Maybe in the envelope was the cure for multiple sclerosis or the answer to what to do with my life now that I wasn't working. Maybe the information included real answers to real questions right under my fingertips and I missed it because I had just thrown it on top of the pile. I dug the packet from Yale Colonist out and really glanced at it this time. If there was helpful information included within the envelope I certainly couldn't find it.

Thankfully, I did take advocate Ada's advice and taped her number to my refrigerator just in case. Several months later, I did need her and Yale Colonist's help with a question. I had received my new insurance card and there were some changes I didn't understand. I asked advocate Ada what the changes meant.

"Oh, that's not really the kind of thing I can help you with. I'm here to help you with any medical and emotional issues you may be struggling with at this crucial time. Is there anything that you would like to discuss that you may be having trouble with?"

"I'm having trouble understanding what my new insurance card means. That is what I am struggling with. How can we get that question answered?"

Advocate Ada needed to place me on hold and then sent me to the main switchboard of the company where I needed to push all the right prompts before I got to a live person who could tell me what the new notations on my card meant. That agent said that there was just a standard update to my insurance plan, no cause for concern.

"Are you sure?" I asked. "I'm worried about this 'tier three' thingy and the note about the 50 percent co-pays. I have never had that before and I take some pretty expensive medications."

The agent said she looked over my prescriptions and I would be all set; she didn't see anything on the list that would change my co-pays. I thanked Yale Colonist for their assistance. The next month when I called my mail-order pharmacy to refill my usual MS injections, I was told to hold, I would need to talk to an operator before the prescription was mailed out. The operator came on and asked me how I wanted to pay my co-pay, as it had increased from its standard three dollars per month.

"Well, I guess you can just bill me like usual. How much is it now?"

"Two thousand two hundred dollars for a one-month supply."

"WHAT?"

I didn't refill the prescription at that time. I called Yale Colonist and was told how I had been sent a new card that explained the co-pay increase. I told them I had called before and asked for specifics and was told that nothing would be affected on my prescription list.

"You needed to have them look at your record directly before they answered that question," the agent stated.

"I did."

I asked to talk to advocate Ada. I was put on hold and sent through a whole series of prompts again before advocate Ada came on the line. I told her my plight. She again told me that she couldn't help with financial issues like co-pays but was available to help me cope with any medical or emotional issues I may be struggling with as a result of my MS diagnosis.

"Ok, my emotional issues are that I am terrified about how I am going to pay these outrageous co-pays for medication I need as a result of my MS diagnosis!"

Advocate Ada offered to transfer me to an operator who could better explain the changes to my co-pays. I hung up. One month, twenty phone calls, and three letters later, the state helped me obtain new insurance and I was able to fire advocate Ada and Yale Colonist. But I thank them for their support.

MS AND THE NIGHT VISIT

What I remember most of the summer is hiding out in my bedroom cave, sleeping, and making calls to try and sort out my life. I must have been writing a bit, as when the summer was over my computer had pages on it that I must have created at some point, but I have no recollection of typing. My mom heard about a writing conference nearby, so I applied for and won a scholarship to one of its classes. It took place the third week in August, which was also when my friend Samantha came to visit, bringing her three-year-old daughter, Lexi, and her fabulous mother-in-law, Barbara. I was looking forward to spending time with all of them and figured with all the sleeping I had been doing in the previous weeks, I should be well rested for their visit.

The conference lasted a week, and it was fantastic. I met many new friends, and the class gave me the confidence to think maybe I could actually be a writer, not just tell people that I was in order to say something when asked what I did for a living. The experience was my first boost toward a potential future. That was the good part.

The bad part was that it was held in an old-fashioned resort area spread out over several blocks, with extremely limited parking and no air conditioning or ventilation of any kind. Once I was lucky enough to find a parking spot, I wasn't getting another. And upon receipt of the scholarship, they asked me to help out at the registration desk which was at the opposite end of the campus from the building where my class was held. Several blocks should have been no problem for me. As inactive as I was, I always outwalked my friends to the point where they would beg me to wait up and be lagging behind while I had no idea why they moved so slowly. But with the heat and the exhaustion that sticky summer, I was a mess. I made it to the registration area that first day but had no idea how I would be able to continue at the conference all week.

That first night of the conference was also the first night of Samantha's visit, and she wanted us to go out to dinner. It was a tradition when Samantha came home to go to the best seafood restaurant in town. It was also a mistake. Being so good, it was always packed. Being always packed, it was also loud, very loud. That night was no exception. Kitchen sounds, server sounds, noise from the bar upstairs and people coming and going from the bar upstairs and a large, crowded dining room added to the commotion and racket. It was just a Monday, but a Monday at the height of the tourist season on Cape Cod.

Lexi was a great dinner companion but that was not the case with the other young ones in the room. The busy restaurant sounds were likely annoying to some of the diners, but with my exposed nerve endings, the noise was downright painful. My head began to rattle and hurt like it had never done before. I felt terrible for Samantha and Barbara, who were treating me and another friend to a belated birthday celebration. It was an expensive dinner and not only could I not enjoy it, it was making my head want to explode. It was all I could do not to rush out before the main course. Why hadn't I thought of this and picked a different place? It had never occurred to me to veer from tradition now that the circumstances had changed. I downed Aleve and hoped for the best.

I do remember a conversation at dinner about Lexi learning to test the waters and starting to cheat or change the rules at games to suit her. I described how I had done that at age five with my Nana Sousa. Nana and I were very close. She didn't speak English but I learned Portuguese as we were always together. By the time I was six, she had moved back to Portugal and when I saw her again, she was stricken with Alzheimer's. I had lost all of the Portuguese language I had learned so there was little communication between us from then on. She died from complications of the disease when I was in my twenties. My memories of her were sparse, but cherished.

I told my dinner companions, as best I could with my head pounding, how I had taught my Nana Sousa to play Candy Land and then figured since she didn't speak English, she wouldn't know if I was cheating. My childish brain didn't think she could understand that it was wrong to move six blue spaces when the card only had two. She caught me and loved me very much but knew she had to call me on my cheating. She said something like, "nao facas isso filha," which I understood at the time to mean something like, "You're cute, but not that cute. Don't try to pull that with me, my little Ivoninia!" (For the record, the actual translation is "don't do that, daughter.") Even Nanas have to set limits. Samantha and Barbara agreed.

My dinner companions and I finally left the restaurant. All I wanted was to be in my quiet home. The main drag was packed and crowded and raucous as usual, and I apologized for cutting out on the night so early. I drove home with the windows down and no air conditioning as I didn't think I could handle the low hum of the motor.

In the car, I noticed that my friend Dora had left me a message. I called her back wanting to chat, to vent my feelings about this frustrating buzz in my brain to my friend, and my guilt for not enjoying a fancy dinner bought for me. But when I called her back, Dora, who had a very busy life, was taking her dishes out of the dishwasher and with the clanging of the pots and pans, I couldn't understand her. I wasn't even able to form the words to explain that I wanted to talk but needed the quiet because of what was going on in my head. She asked me something routine— had I talked to Mya lately or something like that—and I wasn't able to answer. Even simple words like "yes" or "no" were not forming. I hung up suddenly without an explanation.

What I was going through was a fairly typical symptom of MS, but describing what was going on in my head was difficult. Sometimes I describe it as "bleeding in my brain," though I don't know why, because it isn't actual bleeding in my brain. It feels so serious that that very serious imagery is what comes to me when I try to explain it. It was a headache, but not merely a headache. My brain was rattling and humming with a loud, obnoxious noise that I couldn't shut off or shift focus away from. This caused my whole body to feel like it was shaking. I couldn't think or feel anything but this horrible buzzing and drilling in my head, on top of the pain. It had happened several times in the past, including at least three times during my last week at Dr. T's, but this one was the worst.

I went to bed but it was hard to rest when I was like that. I tossed and turned for a couple of hours. TV was not an option, since the lights and sounds were just too much. Reading was not an option, because I couldn't focus on letters, let alone whole words or be able to process anything on the page. I thought of saying prayers to help my head calm down, but I couldn't form the words. The only thought that came into my brain somewhat clearly was the memory of the Candy Land game with my treasured grandmother.

Somehow I came up with the idea to say the rosary. Maybe the rosary would help as the prayers were rote and wouldn't require any actual thinking to say them. It did help and after a few minutes, I drifted off to sleep. Suddenly, I jolted up in bed. The lamp on the other side of the bed was on. I never used that lamp. I knew three things: my name, the fact that no one had broken in, and that the light was NOT on when I was saying the rosary. I don't know how I knew that no one had broken in, I just did. But there had to be a reason for the light. I believed in spiritual visitors, but in spiritual visitors visiting someone else.

It was one thing to believe in it, another to accept it as happening.

The light was a touch lamp. Could I have knocked a pillow into it in my tossing and turning? My pillows were not out of place and if that had happened, they would have miraculously jumped back into their proper place against my headboard. Still, I experimented throwing them at the lamp in various violent sleeping poses. They didn't even come close. I had a problem with mice that summer. Could a mouse have crawled across the nightstand and hit the lamp? But there were no droppings around, and even in my ragged state earlier, I had taken off my jewelry and meticulously lined it up as I always did in front of the light. All the pieces were still lined up. And there were no scratching sounds or footprint patterns in the dust on the nightstand.

Someone was letting me know they were around. Nana Sousa had been devout. Had the rosary and the strong memory called to her? I couldn't say for sure, but I was also starting to realize the horrible rattling in my head had stopped. And I wasn't tired. Now that my brain was back to normal, I was thinking clearly. I lay on my left side and looked out the window as a wild thunderstorm started. I have always been one of those people who believe that if the weather wants to kick up a bit of action, it's worth checking out. It was about 2:30 in the morning. The storm kept me company for three hours as I watched the sharp lightning and listened to the thunder, fascinated.

The only sleep I got that night was in the minutes between the rosary and the light coming on without any known earthly help. But the next morning, I wasn't tired. This was new. Usually I was tired all the time. I was often so tired that I would sleep for ten or more hours, take a heavy dose of caffeine, and still have to struggle to stay awake on the drive to work. But that day, I wasn't.

I went to day two of the conference with new energy. But this time I used my handicapped parking placard, the one that I had finally broken down and applied for. I hadn't gotten it to lend to Chris, despite his request. What made me actually seek out the placard was the arrival of summer and the fact that with a handicapped placard, I could receive discounted parking in my hometown. I didn't like to use the placard for any other reason as it seemed that there were people who needed the special spaces more than me. I didn't like to admit that MS sometimes made it tricky to walk long distances. I wasn't at that point yet. But to save a dollar or two, I was all for it. Somehow, though, I felt it was okay to use at the conference in order to avoid the long walk in the heat. That was what it really existed for, right?

The start of that week reminded me that things were different in my world, it was okay to use things that might be helpful, and that I wasn't alone: a higher being had my back and could send a little extra energy when I needed it most.

PUMPKIN FUDGE

After my self-exiled summer of refuge in my bedroom cave, I emerged anew. There was still paperwork to sort through and plenty of calls to continue making, but it was autumn now. The miserable humidity was diminishing. If fatigue was my problem, then I had rested all summer and maybe caught up on sleep a bit. The last two and half months had been mostly a blur and I was ready to get my life back. I would get healthy and then become a productive member of society.

First up, exercise. The Wii and I had stopped communicating. It refused to forgive me for not even doing the simple balance games over the summer, and I had given up trying to win back its affections. It was not interested in the chocolate I proffered, so I consumed it myself. I had shared the Wii with Lexi during her visit, but as she was only three, she didn't understand the system and the Wii grew even more resentful. It didn't appreciate that I was passing it off to a child who did not perceive its greatness. I did not know how to send a computer in my TV flowers, and, as I had so many other things to think about, I moved on. Not without first suffering extreme guilt at leaving behind my emotionally needy fitness equipment that truly wanted to be with me but was a little too high maintenance for my taste. I needed fun and excitement without demands and commitment. I wasn't ready for the responsibility that came from my on-again, off-again relationship with the Wii. Funny, my sudden desire to meet up with some of my ex-boyfriends for a cold beer.

Fall is my favorite time of year and the weather was beautiful. I would go walking, less pressure. There was a route around my neighborhood that I had previously calculated to be approximately three miles. When I calculated it again, it had shrunk to just under two. How did that happen? Did the neighborhood shrink? Or had my eagerness to get fit in mind and body increased the calculated memory? It didn't matter, it was walking nonetheless.

I set out and at the end of my road turned left to follow my regular path. As I did so, I walked directly into a woman walking a horse and a goat. No, that is not the start of a joke. The horse wasn't that big, and with my left turn we were eye to eye, with only inches separating us. I was taken aback but didn't know if the horse understood "excuse me," so I said instead, "Aren't you beautiful?"

Apparently, that was the wrong thing to say. The woman walking her said sternly, "And this is her goat!"

I guess it was rude not to acknowledge the goat but my cognitively limited brain wasn't fast anymore. All I came up with in response was, "Oh, hi, goat."

The trio passed and went on their way. I walked backwards for several steps trying to make sure the encounter wasn't just part of my MS confusion, and that the goat wasn't too offended by my rudeness.

I had seen rabbits and a large deer in my backyard. I had also observed a neighborhood fox on a nearby road and had been warned about coyotes at dusk, so I thought maybe I should vary my walking route. If I had a tendency to be rude to goats, I didn't want to take any chances with wilder creatures.

My next walking venture was down the main street of my hometown, Provincetown. The wildlife there was just as unusual as a horse and a goat together on a leash, but relatively safer than coyotes. As I walked along the main street, I happened by a candy store that was offering free fudge samples. I had worked in the Cape Cod candy industry as a teen and had long since lost my desire for fudge and taffy. But I was now very attracted to the word "free," and I was exercising, after all. What could a little sample hurt? I would walk it off. The sample was pumpkin-flavored and it was good. It had a nice fall flavor that actually snuck a bit of fruit into my diet. There seems to be some debate on whether pumpkin is a fruit or a vegetable. I don't like to argue so I figured I would just count it as both. I got in one serving of each, just while I was walking. This was great; I could do this healthy stuff.

The sickeningly sweet feeling that overtook me as I walked back to my car made me realize that maybe this wasn't the best way to go healthy. As the commercial strip started to settle down after the busy summer season, there would be lots of other free-bies offered and I couldn't rationalize all of them as partially healthy. Plus, it was a thirty minute trip to Provincetown and gas was expensive, so this really wasn't an answer.

I walked the beach several times and then braved another foray around my neighborhood. On that trip I found a walking stick the perfect size for me. It was a long tree branch lying on the side of the road that seemed to insist "you need me." I picked it up and began walking with it, feeling a little like Moses in *The Ten Commandments*. What I looked like was probably an idiot trying to look like Moses in *The Ten Commandments*, but I was walking and now had protection against any dangerous critters. Plus, I had researched goat etiquette and would be better prepared if I encountered my four-legged friends again.

Next in the get-healthy plan was the veggies. I had put them off long enough, and one small free sample of pumpkin fudge would not satisfy my vegetable requirement for more than a few days. It was time to take charge. A new friend told me about a vegetable soup that was so delicious you didn't even know you were eating vegetables.

"Really? How is that possible?" I suspiciously inquired.

"I'm telling you, it's the best. I don't like veggies much either, but I LOVE this soup."

I actually liked soup; it reminded me of the cooler weather I was looking forward to. She persisted, and I had a get-healthy plan, so I copied the recipe and hit the store. The recipe said you could mix and match which legumes to use, but as I had a plan and her great taste insistence, I got them all. Pretty much everything that had a color and came from dirt went into my shopping cart and came home with me, almost fifty dollars later. For the record, cookies only cost about $2.49 and a box of macaroni and cheese costs less than a dollar, but apparently they aren't very healthy.

Their packaging also doesn't attract bugs. With the fresh-from-the-earth produce in my recyclable bags (chosen to save the planet and ten cents off my shopping bill now that I was a saver) also came a ton of little fruit flies. But I hadn't bought fruit, I had bought veggies. What was this about? I tried to ignore them as I started washing, peeling, chopping, slicing, sautéing, and boiling away. It got warm in my kitchen so I opened my sliding door. A hungry squirrel peeked in through the screen. That had never happened before. I guess my neighborhood squirrels were either drawn to fresh produce or just shocked that I had bought some.

"Sorry, Mr. Squirrel," I said. "I would love to feed you but I need to save money and this soup is expensive. Plus, I need to get healthy. This is all mine. I am going to love it and eat it for days and days and then freeze it and have it again and again so I can be healthy. Isn't there a leaf or a pine needle out there for you to munch on?"

It actually smelled good. When it was done, I got a bowl and a glass of water (I was going all out on this plan—no more Diet Coke for me!), and almost threw up on my first bite. It was not delicious at all! It tasted like vegetables! It tasted like a bunch of very expensive vegetables all thrown in a pot and heated so their awful tastes would all mix together. I struggled to get the bowl down. The squirrel smirked and ran off.

Luckily for me, I started seeing people walking through my backyard. I wasn't expecting any people. On closer inspection I saw that it was my landlord, his wife, and a stranger. They were showing their friend the property. I said hello, and they asked if I would mind if they showed their friend the inside of my rental. When I let them in, the friend commented on how good my kitchen smelled.

"Are you serious? I am trying to get healthy and just made this soup full of veggies because a friend told me I wouldn't even taste them, but I can taste them and the soup is disgusting."

"But it smells so good," the friend remarked. "And how can you not like veggies? I love them. It is all I ever eat."

She was, of course, very healthy looking. And my brain wasn't too clouded by MS to come up with a plan to get rid of the soup. *I'd be doing a good deed,* I reasoned.

"Would you like some?" I gave her a super-huge Tupperware container of it to take with her. Then I gave my landlords their own super-huge container as well. They seemed very excited and later I learned their friend was going through a very bad time, had come to the Cape to get away from some very stressful things, and had loved my soup. My MS brain tried to decide if I could list the soup expense as a charity donation on that year's taxes, but that just didn't feel right, even for the new thrifty me.

I had two small bowls left and told myself I would force myself to eat them. I didn't. When I whined about the soup experiment to Dora, she was not sympathetic.

"What did you expect it to taste like?"

"I don't know. I was told it didn't taste like veggies at all. I guess I thought it would be hearty and filling and maybe taste like fall, but not veggies." Then it occurred to me. "Pumpkin fudge," I said. "Maybe a little less sweet, but pumpkin fudge. That's what I thought it would taste like."

This plan was going to be even harder than the shots.

COGNITIVE/
SMOGNITIVE

With the lovely autumn weather came better health, better attitude, and many, many second thoughts. I tormented myself with internal debates such as:

I feel great, there is no reason I am not working.

Maybe I left my job too soon.

Did I really try as hard as I possibly could?

Nice that I gave myself this hot, miserable summer off but it's time to get my life in order.

I'm sure there is something I can do for work.

I didn't stop to consider the fact that my particular MS symptoms relapse and remit, which is why it is called relapsing-remitting multiple sclerosis. Plus, I had been making many serious mistakes at my job due to MS, even before the computer upgrade. The fact that decreasing my work hours hadn't stopped the problem was a minor detail I blamed on the amount of extra work my coworkers would purposely leave on my desk to punish me for not being there one day a week. Though I felt much better, I was sleeping an average of ten hours a night and was still always exhausted.

Since I had heard that sleeping too much can actually make you more tired, I tried setting a specific sleep schedule. It worked great, as long as I didn't plan on doing anything the following day. My increasing lack of focus and my recent decline in organizational skills created an inability to fulfill even the most basic tasks at times.

One night that fall, I had offered to make dinner for my family while my sister Audrey was in town from Florida. As the day progressed, I just couldn't get it together. It was a simple pasta dish, but even just boiling water and opening cans of diced tomatoes seemed overwhelming. They arrived and I said I would start cooking soon. But I didn't. I sat in my living room visiting and insisting I would start dinner any second. But I just couldn't muster the energy. As the late afternoon turned to early evening and my mother's hunger pangs grew, she realized the problem and offered to take us out to dinner instead.

Employment was different, I told myself. It was action for pay, and getting paid would keep me focused and responsible. I had been working since I was ten, sweeping store fronts, selling shells, and hanging out with toddlers while their mothers ran their family store nearby. I did not know how NOT to work. Many other people with MS worked. I could too. I would find myself a job.

Want Ads-

Receptionist needed for front desk of local town building. Must be friendly, outgoing, energetic, and able to take cohesive notes and transcribe minutes at local town meetings. Computer skills and knowledge of Excel strongly preferred.

Hostess wanted for evenings at busy restaurant. Must be friendly, outgoing, energetic, organized and able to handle chaos well. Weekends and some long shifts required.

Looking for library assistant at public library. Must be friendly, outgoing, energetic, and able to stand for long periods of time. Position requires processing of library materials and shelving. Organizational skills and multi-tasking a must.

Chambermaid needed for off season. Must be friendly, outgoing, energetic and fast. Ability to clean several rooms quickly in short time necessary.

The frustration was coming back. Without a doubt I could pass the friendly and outgoing requirements. It was the other ones that were a problem. Computer knowledge, energetic, organized, long shifts, and standing all seemed slightly problematic. Plus, it was fall on Cape Cod, right when the jobs were winding down. I had been excited about the library job as I had worked in a library before. But I wondered about standing for the whole shift and if I was really tired on a workday, would the shelving be done right? I knew from experience that mis-shelving one book could make it lost forever.

I tried to come up with my own job ideas, including jobs I had done before. Nothing seemed likely. I started to remember the brain fog that would show up from time to time and wondered how I would possibly be able to explain it to an employer, as I was having trouble explaining it to my friends. Hell, I was having trouble explaining it to myself! But I refused to give up, so I kept looking for the position that would be just right for me and my MS.

In the meantime, I received a call from the Writer's Center that had given me a scholarship back in August. I had promised to volunteer for them after the conference if they had any projects they needed extra help with. They did, and this project was perfect for me. It wasn't a paid position but maybe it would transform into something I could do for a company later. All they needed me to do was call all the schools on the Cape, ask them several questions, and put all the answers down on a list for the center, all from home and on my own schedule, when I felt my best. They would soon be offering a writing program for students and needed the contact information for all local English teachers, principals, guidance counselors, and curriculum directors. The Cape is pretty small, but when you factor in public, private, and charter schools, the numbers add up.

I was given several weeks and could set my own hours. I could use my friendly, outgoing skills to the max and I hadn't yet totally given up on my organizational skills. But it didn't go as easily as it should have. I would call a school, ask the questions I needed to ask, note the information, and hang up. When I looked at it again I would see that I had forgotten a question or two. Maybe I had noted the principal's name but was not sure the number listed was his number or the number for the guidance counselor; or for the junior high or high school, for that matter. It would take several calls to one number just to sort out round one. When I finally got to round two, the part of the job that required me to type this all up for the center, I often had to call several of the schools back. I finished and thought I had caught most of the mistakes, but frustration set in yet again. This was a basic job that I had a month to complete and did only when I felt at my best and only for short periods of time. How did this bode for my future in the job market?

Dr. M and I discussed what seemed to be problems with my cognition. She referred me to a famous Boston hospital for something called a neuropsychological evaluation at the hospital's Division of Cognitive and Behavioral Neurology. This was designed to be a four-hour test in a low-stress environment to figure out how screwed up my brain really was. I questioned how it could be low-stress as just the idea of trying to get into the heart of the city was freaking me out and exacerbating everything. I came up with two methods.

1. I would ask my friend Kristin to take me. She didn't mind driving in Boston and I had driven her to a doctor's appointment several months ago.

2. I would drive myself most of the way and then take the subway system into the city. I had taken the trains when I was in college. I could figure it out again, cognitive difficulties be damned!

I had pretty much decided on the second plan, since I didn't like to ask anyone for anything. I would take my chances on the train. My wise mother had her own method to get me to the appointment. She called my dad and asked him to take me. He called and asked why I hadn't asked him. I told him of my train plan and that I didn't want to bother him. He said he would take me. He took his friend to the hospitals in Boston all the time and knew right where it was.

We left before 6:00 in the morning in order to stop for coffee and be prepared to sit in the Boston traffic. We took my little Corolla as my dad's truck was acting up. I grabbed some CDs for us to make up for the fact that my car lacked my dad's awesome Sirius Satellite radio. The good thing about my dad being the better driver of my parents and thus the better parent to be stuck driving me, was that my dad also had better taste in music. I could relate to his Elvis and Johnny Cash and he could appreciate my Rolling Stones and Tom Petty. But we didn't listen to music. We just talked. Or, I should say, my dad talked. I listened and commented here and there, but with my dad he is almost always the one doing the talking. But it worked and was the start of what would become a regular bonding time, with him insisting on driving me to most of my appointments even when I felt I could drive myself.

At one point a friend of his called and my dad answered his cell in Portuguese. It was nice to hear my dad speaking his native language, even if I didn't understand anything he was saying. I told him so.

We got to the hospital in plenty of time but almost got killed twice looking for a parking spot. That was the thing that terrified me about city driving, not knowing where you were and people not allowing you any time, space, or distance to figure it out. My dad didn't even flinch, shades of his years as a police officer driving the cruiser through the pedestrian- and bicycle-clogged main street of a tourist town.

With the car parked, we then needed to find the entrance. There were few signs and every door seemed either locked or for employees only. Eventually we did find where we were supposed to enter, and once there, found a tiny sign with directions to the particular office we needed to get to. I wondered if finding your way to the right office was part of the testing. If you can actually find the neuropsychologist, you will get an automatic C+. The hospital building was antiquated, in disrepair, and depressing. The waiting area had no TV, and the magazines were almost as old as the plaster falling off the walls in the bathroom. When the doctor confirmed that the test would be a full four hours, my dad decided to go visit his brother and sister-in-law, my Uncle Eduardo and Tia Lucia.

The most Portuguese of all my relatives, Uncle Eduardo and Tia Lucia were elderly and kind. Walking into their home in Somerville was like walking into my Nana Sousa's house when I was a kid visiting her in the Algarve. I had wanted to visit Tia Lucia and Uncle Eduardo too and thought we might go to their house after the test, depending on how I was feeling. But for the earlier part of the long day, it was the best place for my dad to hang out. If he waited for me at the office he would go crazy from boredom and the receptionists would go crazy from my dad talking to them the whole time. Everyone would need cognitive testing.

The doctor introduced me to her assistant and we started the process. After some brief questions she showed me a drawing and asked me to write in paragraph form what I saw. I thought this was likely a simple exercise to show off my most basic grammar and spelling skills. I had just told her the only career path I could conceive of was becoming a writer. I had to prove that it was at least a possibility. I asked how much time I had. She told me to take all the time I wanted. Did that mean the entire four hours? I think she was expecting a basic description of woman doing this, child doing that, etc. But I saw a whole story in the drawing and wrote it, complete with a dramatic subplot and a commentary on the decline of a simple moral compass in current technology-dependent middle-class America. Eventually the doctor asked me to stop. Her report on the testing noted: "narrative handwriting sample was creative in content." Perhaps I should have asked for it back to see if I could publish it. I needed the money, after all.

From there, things went downhill. Her assistant took me into this tiny room where she proceeded to have me memorize, spell, associate words, disassociate words, dissect words, add, subtract, remember, repeat, and any other thing you can possibly do to someone's brain. Slowly my head began to expand. Just remembering the test is bringing the awful headache back. The final report shows I tested pretty well but it didn't seem so at the time. At one point, I could not tell the assistant the name of our president. Instead, I said, "I can't believe this, I love him. I voted for him. I can see him in front of me and can see his family. He has a weird name but is a good guy." My Republican friends said that this memory loss was because my brain was blocking out disturbing thoughts.

The part of the test I did the worst on was identifying something missing from a picture. Maybe it was the artist in me altering common perceptions, but they would show me a picture and ask me what was left out. I couldn't tell them and would say, "Nothing, everything is there." The assistant would insist something was definitely missing. Then, to make her happy, I would make something up. If it was a picture of a puppy, I would say a little boy. Every puppy needs a little boy to hang out with. And the assistant would begin writing in her notepad. One picture was of a leaf, what could possibly be missing from a picture of a leaf? A leaf was a leaf. But the assistant would state, "No, something was definitely missing," and we would start all over again.

One picture was of a mother and son walking on the beach. I grew up on Cape Cod. If something was missing from a beach picture I should have known what it was. I kept guessing—a fishing boat, tourists, whales, a keg of beer, sandcastles, nude sunbathers, seaweed, litter, suntan lotion, a cooler, shells, keep off the dunes signs, jaws, park rangers. The assistant scribbled away.

When the four hours of testing was finally done (and they weren't kidding, it took all 240 minutes), I had trouble seeing straight and felt like I was barely walking. I was hungry and thirsty and wanted to take a whole bottle of Aleve but felt I should have food first. There was no cafeteria or even a beverage cart in the whole building, and the water from the water fountain tasted like metal. I gagged. My dad, back and flirting with the busy but trying to be polite receptionist, escorted me to the car. It was now close to rush hour. There was no way I could handle a visit to my Portuguese relatives and my dad thought it was best to get out of the city as soon as possible.

"Ok Dad, but I'm really thirsty and need something in my stomach so I can take a couple of pills. As soon as we are out of Boston can we please stop and get some food? I don't care where or what kind of food, crackers and water even, anything."

He said he knew a nice restaurant we could go to. A nice restaurant meant sitting down and more chatting. It was the last thing I needed, but I didn't want to hurt his feelings.

How had I not noticed on the way up that my dad drove my little Corolla like it was his truck or a heavy police car? The car jolted constantly in the nightmarish city traffic, quickly accelerated to get two feet ahead, then suddenly stopped at the next jam. My head just wanted to explode, and I was convinced I was going to throw up.

My dad got another call on his cell. This time it was from someone he went to school with in Portugal and hadn't talked to for years. Did I mention that the weird thing about the Portuguese language is that it is always spoken in decibels several degrees higher than normal? The volume of the language then increases considerably depending on the excitement level of the speaker. In my mind, Portuguese was booming through my car at a volume loud enough to be heard in Europe. It didn't sound so pretty anymore. We stopped at the side of the road so my dad could write down this friend's phone number and I stumbled out of the car into the rainy rest area. I paced, trying to calm my taxed mind and release the inner screaming that was mingling with the foreign conversation in my car and the roar of the semi-trailer trucks on the highway. The bleeding in my brain feeling was with me and it was strong and painful.

My dad motioned me to come back. He had hung up with his friend and had called Tia Lucia to tell her about this long lost soul he just heard from. She wanted to talk to me.

"How are you, sweetheart?"

"I'm OK, Tia."

"Ay, my Yvonninia, all the time say OK, OK, OK. I say prayers for you."

She started to cry. I tried to tell her really, I was fine. She kept crying. I asked about her and Uncle and she told me they were fine. When I hung up I asked my dad what he told her about my doctor's appointment.

"I just told her I dropped you off at the hospital for some very serious tests on your brain."

"Jeez, Dad, no wonder she's crying."

He must have seen how pale I looked and asked if the Burger King sign he saw up ahead would do instead of the fancy restaurant. He did not like junk food and never wanted to admit any of his kids might like it either. He had likely had a full Portuguese feast at Tia Lucia's.

"Burger King would be OK," I told him. "I could deal with Burger King if it is the easiest."

I had yet to openly admit my junk food addiction to him. The fact was I would have eaten anything at that point. If there had been a farm stand in the rest area it would have been an excellent time to get some healthy food into my system.

It was the best Burger King meal I had ever had. A Whopper Jr. and a couple of little pills later, I started to feel like my head might not explode after all. I went home and went to bed for a couple of days.

Three weeks later the doctor called and said she had the test results. She told me the MS had caused my brain to slow down a bit. She compared it to her elderly father who didn't have dementia, but whom she had to speak to slowly so that he would better understand her when she was telling him something. She said my brain was like that, an old man's. She also told me that I should accept that my multi-tasking skills, skills I once prided myself on, were pretty much shot. I would now have to realize it might take me longer to process things, especially since the test was done in a controlled environment. Exhaustion, stress, and noise would likely increase my symptoms. She recommended that I visit a vocational specialist, whatever that was, and that I only work part time.

She wouldn't tell me what was missing from the beach picture as she said someday I may need to do the test again.

The breakdown of the test results seemed to be that cognitively, I wasn't a total mess—I was just an old man. Good to know.

HEY MS,
HUG THIS!

At some point, I began to understand how a lot of things in my past fit into this post-diagnosis MS world. My whole life had been a mixed bag. During my school years I was a nerd and somewhat cool at the same time. I was responsible but fun-loving, social but only slightly. I was the student whose answers you liked to go over if you hadn't done your homework but also the one you would invite to your Friday night party, if you remembered. In my twenties, I enjoyed the party life and prided myself on being my best at my little summer gift shop job when I was still hung over after only two hours of sleep. Friends thought of me as a drinker even though I didn't really like the taste of hard alcohol, the Allen's Ginger Flavored Brandy and Jack Daniels of my teen years partying with people way too old for me notwithstanding. Life was a constant sway of dependability and slack. I somehow graduated Magna Cum Laude from college even though I really didn't want to be there and had no plans for my future other than to return home to my gift shop job and hang out at my favorite dive bar. This mix seemed to serve me well.

The first obvious sign of the shift changing was in my late twenties and I was reunited with yet another 'one who got away' ex-love. The guy was kind, handsome, and cool. And he liked his partying. I could keep up, but barely. Sadly, we had broken up and he returned home to another state—the story of my life when it came to men, it would seem. When he returned a couple of years later, we flirted with a return to our old relationship. By then, I had a super-responsible job working with crime victims in the court system and lived in a very responsible apartment complex. Describing my life, I told him how I felt when I came home from work one day and saw a bunch of twenty-year-olds moving in.

"It was crazy. My first thought was I hope these kids don't think this is a party place! Then I was immediately horrified at my-self, thinking where did that uncool old lady thought come from?"

I had told him this silly story thinking he would find it amus-ing. He did not. I could tell immediately by the look in his eyes that our lives had too drastically shifted apart and we would never be together again. That night was the last time we ever saw each other.

What do things like boyfriends, memories, and balancing par-tying with being responsible have to do with MS? All of them were aging me much faster than I wanted to be aged. And that was completely frustrating! In the months following the diagnosis, all these things started to swirl together in my jumbled brain. It all made relieving, frustrating sense.

Maybe I can't blame my switch to a more reliable lifestyle in my twenties on the disease, but I now knew that multiple sclerosis can linger in your body for years before being detected. Many people (my parents, my new non-partying, professional friends) would say I simply grew up. But in my thirties I actually began to feel older than the cool me was.

It was little things at first. My memory started to be annoyingly shot, causing my early Alzheimer's worries. I would forget words or what I was doing right in the middle of doing it. People would tell me things that I would later deny they ever told me. My friends insisted that it was normal, it happened to them all the time. But it didn't feel normal. My aunt Liliana and I discussed this at great length as she suffered from it too. My Nana Sousa had had Alzheimer's disease, was it possible that we were also in the early stages of it? Then I started being less interested in going out socially. Oh, when something exciting was going on, I could work myself up to it and enjoy myself. But for the most part, staying home with a good movie seemed just as fun. I worried that I was turning into an old lady before my time. Suddenly having to get up to pee a million times a night didn't help dissuade me from these depressing thoughts.

By my late thirties, I was so convinced I was turning into an old lady far too early that I began to state this fact to people. I had noticed Zack around town before we actually met, and even though he claimed he caught me making googly eyes at him, I always denied it.

"I was NOT making googly eyes at you," I would insist. "I just wanted to know who you were and what you were doing in my town, that's all."

After we actually met, he was more the pursuer. He was two years younger than me and I already felt like an old lady, so I balked at dating a younger man. When he asked how old I was I told him that I was eighty-seven. Luckily, he ignored my feeble joke and we started dating anyway.

My elderly weirdness increased. My bladder became more obnoxious and soon I stopped drinking beer. One beer and I would have to hang out near a bathroom for hours, at least. The extreme fatigue came next. Zack and I could never watch an entire movie together. I was always asleep halfway through and would have to finish it the next morning with a cup of my grandma's tea, sweetened just so. By that time, Zack's normal brain had moved on to other things so rarely did we ever enjoy or discuss the movie together. We kept trying though, and even went with friends to see the second installment of the *Pirates of the Caribbean* franchise at a surround sound theater. Amid the bar fights, explosions, and general loud pirate activity, I was asleep. (For the record, I did not fall asleep during the third and fourth versions as the anticipation of seeing Keith Richards on the big screen was enough to keep me alert.)

Next, were the crazy moody swings—happy one minute, angry the next, and sobbing shortly thereafter. Zack and I both guessed hormones but it sometimes felt so out-of-control I was surprised he didn't dump me right then. But he had been warned that I was eighty-seven and laughed off the craziness—once he felt it was safe to return to the house.

Then there was the weirdness that occurred during my favorite weekend of the year.

We rented a place in Provincetown for the Portuguese Festival so we didn't have to commute the thirty-five minutes after drinking and socializing for three days straight. Friday night the festival coincided with my 20th year class reunion and I was pretty excited. Zack had even given up tickets to see his favorite band with his buddies, telling them he and I had plans. The plans were my reunion and him knowing I was looking forward to it. How could I not love him for that even amid my moodiness?

My cousin Ed and his then-girlfriend Sonya were staying at the same place. Zack and Ed hit it off right away and I was already fond of Sonya. I spent that Friday afternoon with a glass of wine by the bay waiting for Zack to get off work and Ed and Sonya to arrive. As excited as I was, I was also sick to my stomach. This strange ache in my gut was ramping up but I was determined not to let it spoil the plans we had.

We went to the reunion and then hung out with Ed and Sonya and laughed a lot, especially at Zack's and Ed's antics as they got together. They both had a twisted sense of humor and loved to play pranks. Ed had the cool prank ideas and Zack had the talent to pull them off. The next day Julie and her boyfriend, Matt, came down and we had a blast. I was with Zack, my cool family, and my fun friends and the pictures of the weekend show us enjoying ourselves. But underneath my smile in the pictures you see this odd grimace on my face as I was trying to have fun through the severe ache in my stomach. I didn't want to be whiny but felt I should explain why I wasn't eating or drinking and was running to the bathroom constantly, just in case. Ed told me to take a laxative already and get it over with. Just great, who had laxatives but all the old ladies I knew? I was pretty sure laxatives weren't the answer to the problem. Julie was convinced I was pregnant and freaked Zack out with the thought. But I didn't think that was it either. I didn't remember any of my friends with kids describing this problem.

Sonya was into holistic medicine and was convinced it was bad PMS. I wasn't. She tried to give me herbs anyway. We cut our Saturday socializing evening short and Zack was a trouper, staying with me even though I told him to go out and have fun. I was awake all night and by morning told Zack I should go to the hospital. Pain or no pain, I insisted on cleaning up first. I popped two Aleve tablets (the start of my long relationship with the drug) and jumped in the shower. Strange thing was, by the end of the shower I was starting to feel a little better. I had been taking some form of pain reliever all weekend and nothing had worked, so on their own, the pills didn't seem like the solution. But the pain was gone, so we went home and back to work on Monday and didn't think about it for a while.

But it did come back, months later and with a vengeance. I tried to describe this particular ache to Zack. "It's like the inside of my stomach is a soapy, wet washcloth. The pain is like huge hands are slowly wringing the hell out of the washcloth and then slowly releasing it, over and over and over again."

Well, that is different, he must have thought, *she did say she was eighty-seven …*

The clumsiness was also prevalent while I was seeing Zack, but as it had always existed, I just called it clumsiness. In a cleaning frenzy one afternoon I removed the computer monitor I was giving to Drew. Carrying it out to the car, I promptly fell over my front door step, badly twisting my ankle. Everyone asked why I didn't have Zack take the computer out for me.

"Because it shouldn't have been a problem," I said.

I had been in a hurry, wanted it done that second, and didn't think I was too old or too weak to handle such a simple task that I had to ask a man to do it for me. The next year, when Zack was out of town visiting family, I was washing my dishes when a glass slipped out of my fumbling hand. One of the shards somehow managed to slice a perfect oval of skin on the outside of my right thumb. It needed several stitches, and as it was a holiday, required my mom to drive me to the ER in a torrential rainstorm. I still have the scar but the biggest problem of that bit of pre-diagnosis clumsiness was that the co-pays from my crappy insurance for that little incident amounted to almost $300, kind of an expensive bit of clumsy.

Sometimes these ailments would come up in conversation with friends. Since they were sporadic, they didn't seem serious; there didn't seem to be anything to do but accept them and move on. I worried that people would think I was a hypochondriac. I truly didn't like to complain, and so I usually didn't bring this stuff up. But when friends, family, and Zack would ask me how I was I would tell the truth and mention briefly whatever little weirdness was going on. Then they would ask more questions and there I was, complaining. But still, there didn't seem to be anything worth seeing a doctor for. Until one evening at a dinner, my friend Dora told us that one of her boyfriend Gene's early symptoms of his cancer was lower back pain, particularly strong in the morning. I had been having that problem too. I attributed it to the two different cheap, lumpy mattresses I had been sleeping on in the last few years.

This scared me. Cancer? Maybe I should get it checked out. My doctor ordered a back x-ray that showed nothing at all, and again, I was convinced that I was having the aches and pains of a woman who was actually eighty-seven. What Gene had was real and terrifying and would eventually kill him. What I had were bizarre issues I was probably imagining and bringing on myself. That's what I convinced myself of, anyway.

It was easy to convince yourself the symptoms weren't real when they disappeared and there was no way to explain them. While the stomach and lower back pain were constant, the symptom of sudden sharp pain was sporadic. So sporadic that I figured I must have imagined it. If it was serious, it would hang around, right? This sensation varied from a stepping-on-a-tack feel to a being-stabbed feel. Odd, since many assault victims say they don't feel pain from a knife attack until they see the blood. I never saw any blood and while this pain hurt, it would last only seconds. Luckily, they were also random and somewhat rare.

But the aches became a regular part of my life the winter I was thirty-nine. If it wasn't a killer headache brought on by what I assumed was pressure at work, then my body was filled with the overall flu-like aches I was becoming used to. These aches seemed easy to explain, as my mom's friend had been sick a lot that winter with what she called a malaise. That seemed a good word to describe the aches, a malaise. An unexplainable, annoying yet minor illness making you feel lousy but not anything to worry about. Like a nagging cold. It was a crazy-weather winter and people were constantly coming into my office with all kinds of coughs and germs and runny noses. A malaise made sense.

There was a malaise alright, a big, ugly, nasty malaise called multiple sclerosis. I am pretty sure that Zack didn't leave the following spring because of my weirdness and hypochondriac symptoms. We both spent a lot of time and tears discussing the breakup and how it came about. My crazy old woman symptoms never came into the discussion. Still, if they were annoying to me I can only imagine how annoying they must have been to someone living with me. Later, of course, I realized all of those issues were not hypochondria but the early symptoms of my strange disease. The peeing constantly was from bladder issues associated with MS. The fatigue stemmed from my body trying to fight its own immune system that was causing the illness. The aches were from spasticity, which means that my muscles were going spastic. The mood swings probably weren't about MS, but let's blame MS anyway. The weird stomach ache was a symptom called an MS hug. A hug? That's what my bizarre, painful, twisting, almost hospital-going, practically ruining the Portuguese Festival event was, a hug sent to me with care directly from the huge MS PAC-Man-looking antibodies in my body. I thought my appendix was bursting, my friend thought I was pregnant, my cousin thought I needed to go to my grandmother's and take one of her laxatives, his girlfriend thought I should consume weeds. But no, it was one of many hugs. Hey MS, hug *this*!

One of the reasons I called myself an old lady during that time was that the weirdness reminded me of my other grandmother, my Nana Mendes. She was always old. Even in pictures of her in her teens she looked old. After my grandfather retired from fishing they opened a guesthouse that she continued to run by herself after he died. But she was always complaining of aches and needing to nap and put her legs up in the afternoons. We kids would go over to help her with the guesthouse and she would have to hold on very carefully going up and down the stairs. It took her forever to be convinced to leave the house and when she did, she would have to hold on to one of us for support. She started falling and passing out unexplainably, and wound up in a wheelchair on the days she didn't feel steady.

With my own weirdness, I was reminded of her. So was Laurie. During my less obvious symptoms Laurie never felt I was a whiny hypochondriac, but she didn't think of MS either. She hadn't had any of these symptoms. As the saying goes, her MS is not my MS and who on earth would ask a doctor for an MRI based on a tummy ache that ruined a weekend? Now that I had my diagnosis, Laurie and I started to think maybe Nana Mendes had had MS too, as the things she complained about were sounding familiar. Perhaps if we had known, we would have been more patient. We thought back then that she gave in too easily to every little ache or pain. It was unfortunately a state I could relate to now. How many unknowing people look at those with MS and think the same thing? Nana Mendes was never diagnosed; her doctor attributed a lot of her ailments to getting older. I had attributed a lot of my ailments to getting older as well. Which is why I went from being a cool, socially outgoing person in my twenties, to a suddenly old lady in my thirties. At forty, I had my diagnosis.

Some people said I should have been angry. But I didn't feel that way. I looked at Laurie, who needed a brace and often a cane to walk, and I felt lucky. So many people have it worse than me. If I kept doing those dreaded shots, I might stay exactly where I was, symptom-wise. It was scary, but on the whole, I never really felt angry. A little fiery once in a while, but mostly not too mad. And the terror I tried to keep in check. Mostly, having a diagnosis was a relief. It proved to me that my symptoms weren't just in my head. I had a reason for feeling old before my time. Relief was the prevailing emotion, at least until major frustration set in.

Everyone in my life was sympathetic at first and proud that I was taking things so well. I tried not to complain and since my mobility wasn't affected, I didn't look sick. Even dear friends began to think nothing was wrong with me. Well, that was just fine, until one of the symptoms did come up. Then I was making excuses. If I felt unable to do something, they thought I wasn't trying hard enough. When I tried to explain why it was tricky, then I was using MS as an excuse. "You can't blame MS for everything," I was often told in regard to my exhaustion, clumsiness due to lack of balance, and my inability to focus on something. I laughed it off when it took me longer to get a joke, or when I had a hard time trying to figure out what was being said when words were spelled out instead of simply stated. If one of my friends asked me in front of her young child, "Have you seen a-s-s-h-o-l-e lately?" I never got what she was saying on the first try. I had to piece it together in my MS brain.

We would be onto a whole different conversation before I figured out what a-s-s-h-o-l-e spelled and which a-s-s-h-o-l-e that friend was referring too. The irony of being an honors college graduate with a major in English who suddenly couldn't spell a-s-s-h-o-l-e was not lost on me. But it wasn't funny when these same friends didn't quite understand the problems this slowness caused at work. Being spacey in a two-minute conversation was funny. Being spacey in a responsible, busy job where people are relying on you and all of a sudden you are twenty steps behind everyone else, not able to understand what is being shoved at your brain, and expected to be forty steps ahead of everyone, is not.

I had trouble driving in unfamiliar, heavily congested areas, an issue I always had which had increased considerably with the diagnosis. My friends didn't get the link.

"Sometimes we just need to step out of our comfort zones, Yvonne," one friend told me. Another said, "Before you go some- where you are not familiar with repeat to yourself 'I will not get stressed, I will not get stressed.' " When I tried to explain that the problem was not that simple, they would think I was making excuses and I would get frustrated and give up. It seemed silly and useless to try to explain that when driving involves making constant decisions (to pass or not to pass, to speed up or slow down, this lane or that one), and when you need to make these decisions quickly, in an area you don't know, with cars beeping at you and cutting you off, and you are not processing everything around you, it's not just about being uncomfortable—it can be downright dangerous. My friends, with their brains processing at normal speeds, didn't get it.

Another friend asked me how I was doing and seemed to really want to know. On bad days I answered this question with "I'm doing okay. I'm hanging in." She pressed me, and so I told her specifics. Then she commented that she wished I hadn't received my diagnosis as I didn't seem to start having symptoms until I was diagnosed. This, after I had recounted the same issues that we had been discussing for years! Yes, if I was feeling any negative emotion, it was frustration. I turned to God to help fight my anger and terror issues, but not my frustration. For whatever reason, I let that simmer.

It didn't help that I still second-guessed myself sometimes. Was the fact that my fingers seemed weak and not able to hold on to anything just an excuse to not do the dishes right now? Were all the mistakes I made on that volunteer project because I wasn't paying enough attention? Did my mom really tell me that story or was it just a dream? Did I just trip again because my legs were weak and my balance was unsteady, or because I am a natural klutz? Overanalyzing everything made me even more exhausted, but I was now so worried about making excuses that I always wanted to double check.

Dora and Mya came down for a weekend visit. One of our favorite things to do was to walk a jetty at the tip of the Cape that reached out almost a mile into the harbor. From there, you could walk to the lighthouse that marked the most eastern spot in the state. The trek could be dangerous, though. A fall on the jetty could crack your whole body against the rocks at low tide or your head at high, causing you to fall knocked out into deep water. Still, we loved the walk and did it often. That particular weekend I didn't feel steady, so I declined. It was a beautiful day and I told them I would enjoy the sun while they walked.

"Go ahead, please. I am very happy to just sit here and enjoy the gorgeous day."

They didn't walk the jetty though and again, I felt I was making excuses. Not steady? What was that? Perhaps I was just being lazy. But an hour later when we were walking on the main street of town my left ankle gave out and I tripped. I didn't go completely down, but had I been on the jetty when it happened, I would have likely been in serious trouble. Was it a sign that I wasn't making things up? That this balancing act I needed to do about "what to do when" was real? Was it MS or just me being clumsy or lazy again? I wasn't sure, but was glad that Dora witnessed the near fall on a flat street. Did she make the connection with the balance issues and my commenting on being unsteady earlier? I don't know. I worried that it would be whiny and obnoxious to point it out.

The biggest frustration was the work issue. Dr. M agreed that I should only work part time. She seemed to feel that with the fatigue I needed to find a non-stress, minimal computer, easy part-time job. I didn't disagree. The problem was you can't live on part-time pay. And, you don't get desperately needed insurance through part-time work.

"But those don't seem like real reasons to apply for federal disability assistance," she said.

"But the reason you feel I should only work part-time is *because of the disability*, right?" I responded.

She wanted me to push myself, not just fall back on assistance. I agreed that I wasn't ready to retire yet, but also wanted to be able to live and keep getting health insurance for my very expensive Chinese hamster ovary cells medicine. I had been working since I was ten and had never shirked responsibilities. I also believed I should give back in some way, so I continued to volunteer. Dr. M said if I was able to volunteer, then I could work. I suppose this is true, but on the other hand, when you volunteer no one freaks if you make a mistake or you sometimes need to back down a bit. I was willing to work. But finding something I could effectively do was the tough part. I mentioned a job taking tickets at a parking lot. That seemed easy enough.

"No, I don't want you out in the elements like that. The heat will not help your MS."

And so it went. I was worried about taking a cash register job even though I had done such jobs many, many times before. But five years before the diagnosis I took a second job at a mall for the holiday season and was not able to learn the computerized cash register. I had no trouble making change, but returns were always typed in on the wrong button, items were logged in the system under the wrong key, and coupons were not put it. Had that been another early sign of MS? The bosses stuck me stocking shelves on the floor and that was it. I was embarrassed but didn't think too much about it.

Dr. M and I eventually decided I would file for assistance, but also go to a Vocational Rehabilitation Specialist. At the orientation they told me to think up my dream job and let them know when I met with the counselor what it was and they would help me find it. So I did. I was writing a lot and thought maybe they knew of a paper where I could freelance and/or a company that needed somebody part time to write their newsletter. I could do that. The counselor told me starving writers were a dime a dozen, so I obviously needed to forget about them helping with that type of work. What else did I want to do?

"Ummm, how about working in reception? I'm pretty friendly."

She told me I didn't need her help to get that job. Probably true, but I didn't know how much I could make with my state insurance, and needed her input on what people with relapsing-remitting MS do for work when they have symptoms that come and go. In orientation, they had said they worked with people with MS all the time … they must know how people like me managed.

"Oh, you'll have to figure those things out on your own."

She was very nice but I was very confused and frustrated and not sure any more what I was doing there. After many calls and different answers, and more hold time and confusion, I did learn that if I got federal assistance and a part time job, I could not make more than forty dollars a month or I would lose my health insurance. But I wasn't angry. Just frustrated.

MISSING TIME

As you may have discovered by now, multiple sclerosis comes in all shapes and sizes. MS symptoms are especially vague. There are the common: fatigue, tingling, and overall body aches, for example. There are the less common: having to pee millions of times in two hours, muscle spasms that cause limbs to suddenly jolt out from one's body, sharp knife-like shooting pains that last only seconds. There is also the hard to explain: swaying like a drunken sailor, the inability to figure out routine issues (like how to count to ten or how to work the remote control), and an extreme lack of focus.

There are also, of course, the weird: nausea for no reason, dizziness for no reason, mood swings for no reason, etc. Then there are the weirder still: itching all over, trouble swallowing, and

182

trouble speaking are some good examples. Various neurologists differ on whether they accept or deny all of the above, and document these symptoms or don't—more weirdness. But if you search MS symptoms on the web, all of the above will appear.

There is yet another category, however—the unexplained and thus unaccepted. I, a simple MS sufferer from a small town, have discovered the unexplainable. I have pondered, researched, experienced, and analyzed the cause of two of my unexplainable symptoms. And without a medical degree of any kind, I have figured out where they come from. I may have to take some time to expand this research to see if it is the cause of MS as a whole and, if it is, what can be done about it. For now though, I feel it is best to share it with you.

The two unexplainable symptoms I am talking about are ear noises and always being late, fifteen minutes late to be exact. Let's start with the first. There is an official name for ear noises and that is "tinnitus." Once I learned that there was a name for indescribable ear noises, I went to the internet to try to describe them. My web searching showed that tinnitus was fairly common and is basically a sound or sensation of sound where there is no apparent basis. Since only the patient experiencing tinnitus hears the sound, it is not easy to relate it to known sounds, although buzzing, roaring, banging, and ringing were mentioned. Researching further, I learned that the accuracy of my translation was further emphasized by the potential treatments I discovered. What stood out loud and clear was that the treatment options include counseling, and several anti-depressants and anti-anxiety medications, including Valium. My interpretation: many people with tinnitus are just plain crazy.

All of this would be well and good for me except I wasn't simply hearing "ringing, roaring, buzzing, hissing, or whistling." I was hearing shuffling, rubbing, scratching, motoring, drumming, welding, and sometimes the sound of a helicopter landing in my ear drum. These occurred mostly at night and absolutely NOT as I was drifting off to sleep while the Discovery Channel was still playing on the bedroom TV. Doctors shrugged it off and didn't seem to be concerned about the auditory variety. Nor did they believe me when I said I was wide awake. At one point, I was convinced there actually was a helicopter landing in my bedroom as the sound that evening was particularly loud and clear. Other times, the ear noise consisted of the sounds of movement as I lay my head on the pillow, almost like the inside of my brain had to settle down and get comfortable before I drifted off. Since I was always so exhausted, the ear racket didn't keep me awake; it just made me further convinced that I was a nutcase as I fell asleep and dreamed of being forever locked up in an ear noise world.

The other too-bizarre-to-be-explained MS symptom I was investigating was always being fifteen minutes late to everything. It started before the diagnosis when I was sleeping all the time. Prior to that, I was the early one. When I made plans with a friend I would be the first to arrive. It never failed. No matter the traffic, the weather, the stress, the plans, I was always the first at the destination, sometimes more than an hour before the other party.

One time I had plans to meet Julie at a sports bar. I, of course, arrived on time, grabbed a table, and waited. I told the waitress I was waiting for someone. When she came by twenty minutes later and gave me a sad little smile, I ordered a glass of wine. Forty-five minutes later her smile, beaming at my lonely self, seemed to say, "You are being blown off, girlfriend. Save face and split."

I sensed her alarm for my pathetic scene and tried to explain I was waiting for a friend, not a date. My friend was never on time. I ordered another glass of wine and wondered if I should just leave. This was before cell phones were popular and Julie didn't have one. Plus, she was coming out of her way to meet me. What if something had happened to her? I continued to wait. Thirty minutes later I signaled for the check, accepting defeat to the waitress who was super-friendly and very sympathetic as she left my two-drink tab. Julie arrived, extremely apologetic, just as the waitress returned with my change. I felt compelled to declare to the whole pub that while I was single, I wasn't desperate. I had waited all that time alone for a *friend*, not a guy.

The point being, I was always early, never late. It was a habit born of hating to rush around at the last minute. I worked better when I was calm and things were in order. At Dr. T's, I was always the first to arrive and the last to leave. It was crucial for me to have the office unlocked, lights and computers on, and phone messages checked before my coworkers and the patients started arriving and coming at me with millions of questions. Without fail, I was at my desk half an hour early as opposed to the fifteen minutes required by Dr. T.

But in the year before being diagnosed, I was slowly starting to arrive later and later. I still made the fifteen minutes before the office opened requirement, but just barely. I would arrive to see confused coworkers terrified I wasn't coming in at all, as they were not used to this behavior. I would rush around trying to listen to cancellation messages on the machine as my coworkers asked where patients were and struggled to turn on the computers and lights. I didn't like it, but I also couldn't explain it. I was getting up at the same time, having my morning cup of tea while I watched the same news program, making my bed by the time the final weather for the week was announced. What happened to that fifteen minutes? I puzzled about this. It was easy to believe that one of my clocks was wrong but I couldn't figure out which. Was it just taking longer for me to get moving, my morning routine bogged down due to the exhaustion?

The real sign of this new lateness being a problem was that horrible trip to Block Island my mom and I took five months before learning I had MS. I was due to pick her up and drive us both to the bus that would take us on our adventure. And, as my mom couldn't be bothered to learn how to operate her alarm clock, I was due to give her a wake-up call. I did, even earlier than necessary as I was up early and getting ready. I left my house in plenty of time to grab some take-out caffeine, pick my mom up, and make it to the bus. There was no traffic on the roads. There was no line in the coffee shop. But I arrived over fifteen minutes late to a very annoyed mother. "Where were you? What took you so long?"

I had no idea. Everything seemed to go according to schedule yet I lost that time and had no explanation. She feared we would miss the bus. As we pulled into the lot, the bus was pulling out. I slowed down while my mom jumped out of the car to stop the bus and I tried to gather my wits, park the car and join her. We made it, but she was angry, I was rushed and confused, and the people on the bus wondered why fellow passengers couldn't get there on time as they had. I did the only thing I knew how to do—I fell asleep. And stayed asleep for most of the trip, but we have already covered that.

After the diagnosis, my perpetual lateness continued. I tried to circumvent the problem by setting my alarm earlier and moving faster. But still, I always lost fifteen minutes. Where did those fifteen minutes go? Laurie also had a tendency to always be late, usually fifteen minutes late. I figured that was due to her poor organizational skills and planning. But I was a planner and organized to a fault. What was going on?

I went to the web and I looked up ear noises and being fifteen minutes late on MS symptoms websites. They did not show up in conjunction with the illness. As I lay down for my eleven hours plus of sleep one night, the helicopter-landing sound occurred. I knew that it was in my ear but it sounded like it was in my backyard. I got up and looked out the windows, but I couldn't see anything. Then I realized the noise had stopped. I got back into bed. The clock read 10:20. But when I got up to look out the window, it had been 10:04. I had just lost fifteen minutes. It seemed as though I had only been looking out the window for a few seconds but it was now 10:20 as opposed to the 10:04 I had noticed when I first heard the sound.

That was when it all made sense. The missing time and the ear sounds went together, and they had a cause after all. They were caused by aliens! They had to be! Aliens would come down and scoop me up in those missing minutes and then put me down again without my realizing what they had done. Then at night, what I would hear in my ear is the effects of whatever the aliens were doing to me. Were they the mysterious cause of multiple sclerosis? Or were they neurologically specified aliens who were trying to cure the disease?

They seemed nice enough. The sounds weren't angry or scary and who needs to always be fifteen minutes on time for everything anyway? They were saving me a lot of waiting by making me always late. Someone else had to wait for me for a change. As for the lousy Block Island trip, perhaps that was their way of warning me not to go.

"Don't go to Block Island, Yvonne! It is going to be a lousy trip and you will be hot, tired, and miserable. All you will learn on this trip is what the island residents do with their waste products. Miss the bus! Stay home in your bedroom cave and sleep and we will keep conducting our noisy experiments in your brain."

Yes, in this world of MS bizarreness, I had finally figured out a plausible explanation for MS symptoms the doctors didn't want to accept as they were just too weird to be explained. Fellow MS sufferers, now you know. What you can't blame on MS, blame on the aliens.

FOGGY BRAINS, SILLY GAMES, AND SHINY THINGS

Next to the exhaustion, the brain fog was the most troublesome symptom for me. And since this is MS we're talking about, where nothing is as it seems, it is one of the hardest to describe. I think the MS professionals are actually referring to brain fog when they mention fatigue, but I am not really sure. I know I wasn't able to explain to Dr. M the specifics of what I meant when I complained about being tired all the time. I said I could sleep forever; she said that is not MS fatigue. I told her I had trouble thinking; she asked me to explain. I tried to explain that I couldn't explain because I was having trouble thinking. She glanced at me as if I was making this up; how could it be so if I couldn't explain it? And so went this particular multiple sclerosis conundrum.

Sometimes I would describe the brain fog as my brain being all fuzzy. In my altered state of focus, a fuzzy brain reminded me of the fuzzy tongue I would get the morning after a night of partying the summer I turned twenty-one. No amount of toothpaste would clear away the fuzzy, icky feeling in my mouth. No amount of focus or meds would clear away the fuzzy, icky feeling in my head on these recent days. At least when I was twenty-one, I had exciting memories the morning after, if I could remember them, that is. Thank goodness I had purchased the computer earlier in the year as I realized it was the only thing that got me through these long foggy hours.

It was around this time (and likely on one of the clearer afternoons), that I made a key discovery, one that would have a great influence on my future and revolutionize the way doctors assessed MS patients. I should have recognized the importance of my discovery long before, when the essential switch happened in my life. No, I am not talking about the initial diagnosis or when I walked out of my job. I am talking about when I switched from playing Solitaire to playing FreeCell exclusively. This may not seem like a big deal but looking back, it really was.

I don't remember how or when I started playing FreeCell but at some point, mindless Solitaire turned into the more advanced version of the game. Oh yes, I dabbled with Spider Solitaire but that was almost as boring as regular Solitaire, only more frustrating and basically creepy. Who wants to play a game that constantly reminds you of a spider? I kept thinking one was on me as I lined up the cards on the computer with my right hand and swatted at imaginary arachnids with my left. I get the heebie-jeebies just thinking about Spider Solitaire.

But FreeCell was different. Unlike the more basic versions of the game, FreeCell wasn't mindless. It took strategy and planning, but not so much it would give you a headache. I could loll away a whole afternoon with the game and it helped me feel slightly more useful than just staring at the ceiling did. When I had tried and failed at the likelihood of accomplishing anything in my day, FreeCell was the answer. Its volume was not as loud as that of the TV or the radio, the thinking required was limited and did not need to be retained, and the cards were large and didn't strain the eyes too badly.

I learned that how bad the brain fog was on a given day correlated directly with how well I played. If I lost game after game, I best keep playing as the brain fog was extreme and wasn't going away any time soon. If I won five games in a row, I knew I had the focus and ability to get up and actually do something, even if it was something small. I didn't want to waste my life in a computer card game world but this seemed to be what worked on particularly foggy days.

I found a website where you could play for free and, if you won, you would get points. You could use the points to enter drawings for cash prizes: fifty-dollar gas card, one-hundred dollar Walmart gift card, twenty-five dollars to spend at Amazon.com, etc. I never actually won any gift cards, but at least I could feel like I was doing something productive on the days when there would be no productivity in my MS world.

Here is what I discovered: lots and lots of people with MS are also addicted to FreeCell. For years, Laurie had a computer that she only turned on in order to play the game. When I asked other MSers, they would tell me that they too, could play FreeCell for hours. Why didn't the neuropsych people just test a patient's cognitive abilities by having them play FreeCell instead of taking all those weird tests? In one hour, a doctor would be able to tell how a patient was functioning just by how well they played the game. Give up four games in a row within thirty seconds? Go to bed and rest. Having a ten-game winning streak? Go attack the mounds of paperwork sitting on your kitchen table. I tried to describe to Dr. M my theory of how understanding the importance of FreeCell in the lives of MSers would be a critical step in understanding their cognitive development, but she wasn't getting it.

Seems the computer game company with the free points did get it, however. In order to play for free, you had to watch a thirty second commercial before each game started. One of the commercials was for another game site that was specifically geared to helping people with cognitive difficulties play games that would strengthen their brain power. That sounded great, so I signed up. I played for free for two weeks. And, like FreeCell, sometimes I played well and sometimes I didn't. Sometimes my focus was right on target and sometimes it was all over the internet. But the games were fun and, who knew, maybe they actually helped. Then my free trial was over. Improving my mental alertness and brain power would cost money I didn't have. I went back to FreeCell.

I discussed my foggy brain issue with my hairstylist. I was long overdue for a cut. I sat in her chair and she asked me how I was. I told her it was one of my foggy days, that I was having serious trouble thinking and focusing. I then asked her to cut a lot of my hair without getting rid of too much, to get it off my face and out of my eyes, but to leave me with long bangs. To layer the sides without adding any layers. To take off several inches but not so much it looked like it had been trimmed. To get rid of the wings, but keep the body. To keep it straight but try to save a few curls. Luckily, she ignored my fog-induced "instructions." She always did what she wanted with my hair anyway and began to cut.

Like many kind non-MSers try to do to sympathize with MSers, she told me that she could relate to my foggy brain problem. Her dad called it shiny-thing syndrome. From childhood on, she described, she was able to focus very well until something shiny would catch her eye and she would be off to investigate it, leaving whatever she was doing in its wake. It made sense when, during my cut, she ventured to another stylist's station to check out her coworker's new engagement ring for the tenth time. Shiny-thing syndrome.

I remembered once taking a quiz on Facebook. The quiz told you what character in the *Wizard of Oz* you most resembled. I was sure I would be Dorothy: sweet, innocent, responsible Dorothy. But when the results came in, turns out I was Toto! I was a yappy, obnoxious dog. The reason the quiz told me that I was Toto was because I was a good friend, fiercely loyal, but was also easily distracted and couldn't resist directing my attention to whatever new thing popped up in my path. Shiny-thing syndrome again.

Was that what the brain fog really translated to for people with MS—shiny-thing syndrome? The problem was, during those low-focus days, whatever popped up in my path to distract me didn't have to be shiny. I could lose the only focus I had just by realizing that I needed to go to the bathroom. Silverware was shiny but that didn't keep me focusing on doing my dishes. I wondered if other MSers suffered from my kind of brain fog or did they only have shiny-thing syndrome. I would ask them, but they aren't able to explain their brain fog either. I would explain it to them, but I don't really know what I mean.

SCARY
MOVIE MEDLEY

About the closest I ever came to describing the brain fog successfully was after one particularly restless day near Halloween. The only thing I felt compelled to complete on that day was getting my stack of dishes done. They had been piling up for a while and I had no other commitments to worry about. *I will feel better when my dishes are done,* I foolishly thought, *then my world will be settled and I can move on to figuring out the rest of my life.*

Since it was rare for me to be up before 10:00 a.m. and I move ever so slowly in the morning, my memories of the day begin in the afternoon. I was shuffling around my house, trying to focus. Ignoring my lists—the to-do-this-week list, the to-do-before-Christmas list, the things-I-should-try-to-do-in-general list and, of course, the things-I-should-try-not-to-forget list, I was determined to get the dishes done.

As I started, it occurred to me that I might have more motivation if I had music going. I dried my hands and headed to the stereo. But then I saw my computer and tried to remember if I responded to that important email I had received the day before. While looking to answer that question, I discovered new emails in my inbox and set to sorting through them. I wound up overwhelmed with the amount of junk emails and chain emails coursing through my web account and gave up, opting to play FreeCell instead.

It was during FreeCell that I became grossed out by the horrible taste in my mouth that my meds were giving me. I got up to brush my teeth and drink some water. Pouring a glass of water, I realized that I had barely started the dishes and dunked my hands in the soapy dishpan. Three plates and barely two minutes later, the glass of water had gone right through me and I ran back to the bathroom. *How on earth am I supposed to drink seven more glasses today?* I wondered as I debated actually moving into my bathroom.

The fog in my brain continued. The only thing I was focusing on was my lack of ability to focus. This is the fog-like state in which I exist on some of my MS days, which makes me think of the movie, *The Fog*. Figures. Leave it to me to equate my multiple sclerosis to a horror movie. But is *The Fog* the right horror movie? I was wandering around lost in my own little world and not feeling quite right, almost zombie-like. Yes, zombies, zombies are a good description. I am an MS zombie for sure. Many days I will stay a zombie until I fall asleep, where I will be alive but dead to the world for at least ten hours. Then it hit me, my MS world is not *The Fog* but *Night of the Living Dead*.

Somehow, thinking of MS in terms of horror movies brought me comfort. *Night of the Living Dead* is definitely the horror movie for sure.

Or was it? Sometimes I just wanted to scream. Actually, I just wanted to scream a lot. Maybe my MS really is *Scream*? I have always been a Neve Campbell fan. But does the movie *Scream* completely reflect all that my MS is to me?

It likely depends on what my MS is doing on any given day. Often, it makes me think I am going crazy. I think of the classic line in *Psycho,* "She just goes a little mad sometimes. We all go a little mad sometimes."

I remembered all the hysterical mood swings and weird symptoms I experienced before I knew I had multiple sclerosis. I remembered all the people in the world around me being totally off-kilter but acting as though I was the one who was screwed up. Like when I had to go to my drycleaner's several times in one week because they had given me the wrong pants.

"Yes, they fit. Yes, they are the same color. Yes, they have the same fashion label and size label. But these pants have cuffs at the bottom hems. My pants don't have cuffs. Yes, of course I would know if they were my pants or not. I will keep them as I need black work pants but one day soon, someone is going to come in and say they have the wrong pants and I am telling you, I have theirs and they have mine. Feel free to call me when that happens and I will exchange them."

My drycleaner and I had this little diatribe over and over. Strange how the other customer never realized she had the wrong pants. Yes, *Psycho* seemed to be the right movie, the one that most described my MS. When I was a teenager I actually waited on Anthony Perkins at a candy store only ten days after seeing *Psycho* for the first time. My friend Heather also worked at the store and had watched *Psycho* with me. She was so freaked out that she ran in the backroom to stifle major screams and call 911. It was left to me to wait on him. I gave him a whole extra half pound of penuche fudge so he wouldn't bring out his knife and start swinging. Yes, *Psycho* felt right.

Bathroom again, but I stopped first to remove the pebble in my sock. But there was no pebble. What was that annoying feeling? And that one, the sudden, sharp jab in my left arm? And that one, the squeezing and releasing of my abdomen as if my stomach were in a vise? And then came those weird ear noises. For what seemed like the millionth time, I worried that my body was being taken over by aliens. That's it, *Invasion of the Body Snatchers*! That is definitely the horror movie that best described my MS. *Invasion of the Body Snatchers* totally explained how aliens had taken over and turned me into a screaming, psychotic zombie living in a deep fog.

Having this serious question answered and finishing up what was likely my tenth trip to the bathroom, I tried again to remember what I was supposed to be doing. Oh, right, the dishes. I shuffled back and plunged my hands into the cold water. As I did so, I felt awkward and completely out of sorts. I was tired, clumsy, and blinking from the glare of the setting sun. Images of *The Creature from the Black Lagoon* began to cloud my foggy, psychotic brain.

Thus, the foggy afternoon turned into a foggy evening and the dishes did not get finished. The day was not completely unproductive however. I did manage to add "buy Halloween candy" to my things-to-do-this-week list.

CELL PHONE CRAZY, CRAZY CELL PHONE

So, if my neuropsych tests show only slight cognitive difficulties increased in times of stress, then why was it that something as simple as a basic cell phone caused me to have not one, but TWO, meltdowns at the cell phone store? Why are the things that are constantly being improved to make life better for most of the world causing such immense problems for people with MS?

Totally unrelated case in point: the town next to mine had two normal-sized, perfectly efficient grocery stores. Then store number one decided it needed to expand to better serve all of its customers. It turned into this incredible behemoth with miles and miles of aisles in its center, filled with crates and crates of groceries to fill its miles and miles of shelves. This made it way too many aisles harder to negotiate and woe to the fatigued MSer who forgot that she needed tomatoes and oranges while she was in the egg and milk aisle. That three mile walk back to get produce just wasn't worth it. Need I comment again on how veggies are very obnoxious and troublesome?

So I switched to the other simple grocery store that had all the basics right where they should be and forgot the now fancy-schmancy grocery emporium. Except store number two decided it needed to expand as well. When it emerged from improving itself, it was now even more obnoxious than store number one. It, too, had added miles and miles of aisles but it also flip-flopped locations of where things should be.

Both stores now placed a chart at the end of each aisle to pinpoint the location of all items, but the chart was always at the opposite end of the aisle from where I was. Ten city blocks down the aisle to find the chart and the item I was looking for wasn't on it. I would then have to search through the maze for someone to help me only to be told that what I needed was located six aisles back. And, since both stores had to increase their prices to pay for their helpful expansions, and the co-pays on my medications were extremely expensive, I would be forced to give up and head to the convenience store. There, I would simply purchase a chocolate bar and a fountain Diet Coke to combat the stress the shopping trip brought on, both for under two dollars and within ten easy walking steps in the store.

"We must keep improving things to make shopping better for all of our customers," the managers say. We MSers thank you for all of these wonderful upgrades.

So why should technology and cell phones be any different? Of course, even before the diagnosis, I was late to the cell phone craze. When I finally entered it, it was due to my job and I had no choice but to learn cell phone basics. And I do mean basics—I'm all about keeping it simple. Driving home one weekend I dialed my sister's number, only to have the phone tell me I was actually calling my nephew. "CALLING DREW" it flashed at me. I almost went off the road. How did my cell phone know who I was calling? When then eight-year-old Drew answered the phone I, now safely pulled over to try to figure this out, asked him how this could be. "How did my cell phone know who I was calling?"

"Auntie, I put my name in your phone when you were home last week."

I didn't even know that could be done, never mind that he had known how to do it. It was my own fault, being so far behind the times. Back in college my mom asked my friends what they thought I might want for my birthday. They told her a cell phone. Personally, I would have said cash and chocolate chip cookies. Indeed, cell phones were the cool gift of the late eighties, especially for a college student traveling on two buses to come home every once in a while. She could tell by my confused and, without meaning it to be, ungrateful expression that the expense and coolness factor of this gift would be lost on me and she returned it.

Years passed and eventually I began to realize that I needed my own personal cell phone like everybody else in the world. I headed to the store to purchase one.

"That's OK," I told the salesman, "I don't need anything fancy. I am just using it for basic calls."

Once I got used to it, I decided I would use it for every call. What did I need with a landline now that I had a cell? The simpler and cheaper the better. Days after I met Zack, my phone started writing to me, sweet, flirty comments as if it wanted to date me. Of course, I had heard about texting but had never done it. I wasn't so dumb, and it didn't take longer than a few hours to figure out that it was actually Zack sending me messages through my phone, that it was he that wanted to take me to dinner, not the phone itself. Then I got my monthly bill and realized text messages actually cost more than dinner and signed up for a text messaging plan. Even though the phone itself was quickly becoming outdated, I was in with technology. On things went in my simple cell phone world.

Recently, one spring afternoon Dora, Mya, and I were having lunch. They started talking about their recent cell phone purchases. Words like smartphone, iPad, tablet, android, 4G, data plan, apps and other complications started to spew from their discussion.

"You guys totally lost me. All I need is something simple, basic even."

They asked to see my phone and Dora, especially, was shocked.

"You have to get with the times, Yvonnie, this thing is so antiquated," she said.

"But it works. What's wrong with it?" I asked.

"Well, look, it doesn't even have a real keypad. It must take you forever to send texts."

"I've gotten used to that, it's no big deal. What can I do with your phone that I can't do with mine?"

"Well, for one thing, you can access the internet any time you want."

"But I bought a $400 computer for $1,200 while I was on my legal speed to access the internet. I can use that."

"But what if you're not home and you want to check your emails? What are you going to do then?"

"I guess I would wait until I got home. Or, if it was an email emergency, I guess I would go to the nearest library."

"But you can take videos with my phone," Dora said.

"I think I can take videos with this one," I replied. "I just don't know how and since I don't need to take any videos, I haven't bothered to figure that out."

"I don't think I can take videos with my new phone," Mya chimed in.

"Of course you can, let me see it," Dora demanded.

She began to try to figure out how to take videos with Mya's phone and proceeded to get frustrated because it didn't seem to work as it should.

"I rest my case," I stated as our lunch began to arrive. "Why do I need to cause myself more frustration when this little phone works out well for me?"

"They don't even make those types of phones anymore. What are you going to do when something happens to it? You'll need to upgrade then."

"I guess I will have to deal with that when it happens," I replied. "And you better not have just jinxed me."

Sure enough, one month later, after one too many incidents of my klutzy, tingly fingers dropping it, my precious phone was dead. There was no CPR for it. I had to let it go. Off to the cell phone store of the cell phone company I had admired since the beginning of time. Well, the beginning of time as in my accepting mobile phone technology into my life, time. I loved the company I belonged to and was so enthusiastic about their service that I could actually do their commercials. They had the best customer service in the world and their fees were far better than the top, more popular carriers.

As they were a smaller company they had fewer towers on Cape Cod and I found a lot of dead zones when I drove around. But I just learned where the dead zones were and didn't make calls when I was in them. As this was my only phone and my home wasn't in a dead zone, life was good. Since I was technologically clueless, I found that I had occasion to call the company often. And each time I did, their super-friendly operators went above and beyond. I had even asked to speak to the managers several times so that the higher ups would know how I felt and commendations would go in the operator's employment file.

During the height of my MS symptoms that I didn't know were MS symptoms (just knew that I was exhausted, depressed, missing Zack, and my life was falling apart), I found comfort in the cell phone operator's sympathetic help. My bills showed that my costs had suddenly skyrocketed and I called the company to see if these high fees were yet another cross I had to bear. I was put on the line with Latiesha. I told Latiesha that I was going through a bad time and had far exceeded my allowable minutes while wallowing on the phone about the state of my life. Latiesha began to ask me therapeutic questions such as: Did I expect the bad times to continue? Was there a regular part of the day that I found myself reaching out to others? Was there a certain group of people I could call regularly?

"Girlfriend," she said, "I know when I am going through a bad time I call my mama. My mama always gets me to snap out of it.

'Latiesha Girl', she says, 'you need to pull yourself together.' Do you call your mama?"

I felt like I was in a counseling session. Then Latiesha wanted to know, if the people I called ever called me back.

"Well, of course they do," I replied. "I'm not a total loser."

Latiesha then went on to design an awesome cell phone plan that allowed me to call whoever I wanted, whenever I wanted, with the ability to text nonstop, all for an extremely low monthly fee. She even came up with little pictures on my phone of the people I called the most. When my mom called, the mom figure on my phone's screen popped up. When Mya called, this glamorous looking Asian model type's picture would pop up, which of course, made Mya very happy. And I didn't have to do anything, Latiesha did it all. When I told Mya how Latiesha had solved all of my problems with her caring questions and I felt better than I ever had before, Mya, who was also going through a crazy time, wanted her number.

"But you don't even use her company as your phone carrier," I told her.

"Does that matter?" she asked. "It sounds like Latiesha can solve anything. I want to talk to her about some things going on with me."

Yes, I loved my mobile phone company. But after Dora jinxed me with all her upgrading talk, I was extremely nervous walking into the store. They confirmed my phone had died and there was nothing they could do to save it. I needed to mourn and move on. What type of new phone did I want? An android, a tablet, a smartphone? What type of things do I do on my phone? I told the salesman that what I did on my phone was talk, maybe text here and there. I didn't need anything else.

"I'll tell you what I would really like," I said. "I would like to turn around and when I look back, have you hand me the exact replica of my phone with all my stuff on it, like I never lost the old one. Can we do that?"

"Ahh, no," he answered. "I don't think they even make these phones anymore. But we can get you close."

When I left the store I had a flip phone that was considered their most basic model available and I actually knew how to use it. I was again so happy with my cell phone carrier that I renewed my contract for another two years. I told him that I was clumsy so he added a protective cover for the phone and asked if I wanted insurance. I told him no, with the hard plastic cover I felt secure and left feeling like I had put the trauma of getting a new phone behind me. *So there, Dora, I didn't need to upgrade after all,* I thought, smiling. My smile did not last long.

The first problem was that I couldn't just text like I would normally text. The new flip phone thought it was smarter than me and would pop out words it assumed I meant. At times I felt MS made me dumb but I still knew what I wanted to say. How come my phone wouldn't let me just say it? I looked up the problem in the little manual. It seemed that if I wanted to write out my text messages like I had always done, I had to change modes. What was a mode? Nowhere in the book did it tell me how to keep the mode from changing back to the mode that kept trying to tell me what to write. I would have to choose from Symbol, Numeric, T9 English (don't let the word English fool you. That's the one that tries to write its own messages) and ABC. Turns out, ABC is the mode I needed. And since I would forget to select ABC each time I tried to do a text, I would have to start again, hit clear several times, change out of English T9 mode, select ABC and then re-type my message, now taking four extra steps to just send the word "Hello" to a friend.

There were also more dropped calls than on my old phone. I wondered if that had anything to do with the little symbol next to the bars in the upper left hand corner of the screen. I looked in the book; it didn't say what that symbol was. Next, every once in a while I would make a call, only to have the person on the other end of the line not be able to hear me even though I could hear them. Back to the mobile phone store I went.

A girl named Betsy told me that the dropped calls and the people on the other end of the line not being able to hear me was due to the lack of towers on Cape Cod combined with the swell of extra visitors. "Reception is always at its worst in the summer. You will find it is better after Labor Day. If it doesn't clear up, bring it back then."

"Hmmmm, my other phone never did that," I said. I then asked about the little picture thingy in the left hand corner next to the bars. "Oh, that must be the data signal; it likely means you are getting data, like a picture text."

"But it's there all the time and changes colors. And I hardly ever get picture texts."

"Sometimes it is just there," she responded.

I asked how to change the text mode so it was always on ABC if I wanted to send a normal text.

"It won't let you change it permanently because the ABC mode is the old, outdated way of texting. It does it this way to make things easier for you. Watch." She then showed me how to write texts in the English T9 mode and how much easier it was. "See, it's a shortcut."

I tried it. I tried it again. It wasn't easier. It confused my cognitively-limited brain even more. My MS brain doesn't like shortcuts. Sometimes it doesn't even like longcuts.

One month later I was back to the store. Now more than ever when I called people they couldn't hear me. Was it too much to ask that I just be able to make a call? Of course, when I got to the store the man working used my phone to call his buddy, and his buddy could hear him. "I don't see a problem," he said. "Nothing we can do if it doesn't do it here."

But that was the point, it didn't do it all the time. I had called the company's main number on my way to the store hoping to talk to Lateisha, but it turns out that they wouldn't let you request your favorite cell phone operator. The company did a thing they called Refresh and the store guy said maybe that fixed it. I had my doubts. His manager noticed that I only had a few bars next to the unknown symbol and that didn't seem right to him. He told his employee to replace the SIM card. "It should be all set now."

I went home and confidently chatted for several days. But less than a couple of weeks later when I made calls I started having people yell at me, "Hello? Hello? Is anyone there? Hello? I don't have time for this! Who's there?"

I would yell back, "It's me. Can't you hear me? Can you hear me now? Can you hear me now?" Click.

Back to the phone store and this time back to Betsy who remembered me. "Hi, what did you think of that texting trick I showed you? Doesn't it make things easier for you?"

I tried to be nice and polite as I told her my problem. She called her buddy. And, of course, he could hear her. The only thing they could do was order me a new phone of the same model for a warranty fee of twenty dollars as I hadn't purchased the insurance. And, as that model was not in the store, it could take up to ten days unless I wanted to pay another twenty dollars for overnight shipping. They could also give me a loaner for a fifty dollar deposit and that I would get back when I brought the loaner back. When I got the shipment, it could only be sent to my home, not the store, and I would have to change the SIM card and the battery before the new version of the same phone would work. No, they didn't know what the problem was. No, they couldn't be responsible for it as they didn't make the actual phone. Yes, I still had to pay the warranty fee. Even though I hadn't damaged the phone I still had to pay for the shipping of a new one.

"Next time just come in right away," Betsy said. That was when I started to cry. I wasn't faking it. The tears were huge and wet and embarrassing. I am not sure if it was the money, the thought that I was going crazy, or that the whole idea of waiting for and then trying to set up a new phone was just too much for me. Just like the new text messaging system designed to make my life easier. Or the grocery stores that gave me a much better shopping experience as I navigated the multiple, immense, and cluttered aisles.

I tried to explain that I did come in right away and that they had given me other reasons why this could be happening. I tried to explain that changing the battery and SIM cards in a new phone was just beyond me. Betsy tried to explain how easy it was to do those things and that I would have no problem. I had no idea what she was talking about. I was humiliated and I didn't want her to think I was a drama queen. So I tried to explain that the reason I couldn't understand anything beyond why people couldn't hear me when I made a simple call, was because I had multiple sclerosis.

I am not sure that explained anything and since this craziness had to be a mistake, I called the company. No Latiesha and no help there. What had happened to all the awesome, kind opera-tors? While I was on hold for ten minutes I looked at all the post-ers on the wall that explained how the company was stepping up to make things better for its customers, how they now put the best technology right at your fingertips for the best in ease and satisfaction, and how they were expanding faster than any other company.

When I finally reached a manager at headquarters and stressed my plight they told me the same things that Betsy had and that I was on my own. Oh, and by the way, my contract didn't expire until spring of 2013 and if I really wanted to leave them it would cost $200. In the meantime, Betsy took pity on me. The store would trust me with their precious loaner without the deposit and they would credit me the twenty dollars to ship the new phone. When I got it, I could bring it in and return the loaner and they would set it up for me.

I appreciated it and, feeling comforted, further tried to explain why I had broken down. All Betsy must have wanted was to get me out of the store quickly, so she said all the kind things you say to people you don't really understand: it's OK, no need to worry about getting upset, people get upset all the time, etc.

She told me the loaner phone was exactly like my current one except instead of flipping, it slides. (It wasn't just like the other one. I could tell that when I slept through an appointment the next day when the phone alarm didn't go off and I could not figure out why. With the fatigue, I always slept through my regular alarm. The cell phone was the one that actually got me out of bed.)

"By the way, what is that picture thing in the left hand corner?" I decided to ask again.

"I'm not really sure," Betsy said. "I'm not used to that phone, they are all so different."

I got my new phone the next week and took it in to have them change the SIM card from the loaner and copy all the old pictures and texts from the old phone to the new one. It didn't work. Betsy tried to copy the old data several times but couldn't tell why it wouldn't go through. She also changed my phone screen to a mountain brook scene that would have been lovely if it didn't make me dizzy, make my eyesight go blurry and hide all the things I needed to see. I couldn't even take looking at the new picture and asked her to please change it. Was I sure that wasn't the picture that was on my old phone? We took it out again to look at. It turned out the old phone did have a picture but it was different and minimized and thus easier for me to look at. She tried to show me how to change it myself. I had no idea what she was talking about. My eyes were getting watery and Betsy hustled me out before another breakdown came on, repeating, "It is OK, I understand. You'll have no problem now."

And I didn't, for ten days. On the eleventh day, I made a call and had a lovely conversation. I made a second call and got hung up on. I tried the number back and heard "Hello? Can I help you? Is anyone there?" I called my mom and heard "Hello. Hello? Yvonne, is that you? I can't hear you! Is the problem my phone or your phone? Hello?"

I called the cell phone store hoping they wouldn't hear me either so when I showed up I would have an actual example of the problem. But that call (of course) went through. Back to the store I went. Betsy was not in, but another manager was. Betsy had filled her in on the problem. No, they had never heard of this before. They really weren't familiar with that model of phone. They can order me another one and if it acts up within ten days then they could give me a different model. They can only order a different type of model if I had tried three of the same models already. Next time, I should come in right away. I needed to let them know as soon as this happens, etc. ...

"Can't you check the website of the company who makes the phone to see if they have any reports of problems with this model?" I asked.

"No," the manager kindly told me. "We don't have internet access here."

I looked around at all the fancy-schmancy phones lying around the store and the phone on her belt that kept buzzing and looked pretty fancy to me. No internet access? Isn't that why Dora had told me I should get one of those fancy models?

"Please tell them when you order a new phone to make sure that if it's not going to work, it acts up within the ten days so I can get a whole different model. Please let them know that I am not trying to con them out of an expensive upgrade, I really only need a phone that works. That's not too much to ask, is it?"

I made it out of the store before the real waterworks started. In my car, I looked at the screen of the phone that now only worked sometimes, to see the horribly busy mountain picture when the tears started again. I took the phone back in and asked her to change it.

"Oh, I did," she said. "I don't know why it put up that other picture. I wonder why it didn't take the one you asked for."

She changed it again. And tried to show me how to change it myself if it kept happening. She showed me again. I nodded at her dumbly and left.

More than the illness, progress was really making this MSer's life difficult. Either that, or the aliens were starting to tick me off …

STOOPING TO
A NEW LOW

A nd I don't mean my posture, which is atrocious. I am talking about the recent incident where I played the MS card in the church confessional. Who's fooling who there? I didn't mean to do it, but it worked pretty well.

Reconciliation and I have always had issues. I could never remember if the light meant the confessional was open or not, or if the Church even still used the light. Twice I walked in on a fellow penitent and humiliated us both. After which I was too frazzled to confess and would either leave or stammer through the whole process. Or I would forget my Act of Contrition. I knew that prayer, of course. With my standard Catholic guilt I actually said it all the time. But in the confessional I would often forget and the priest would have to help me through it, making me feel like a fraud.

"I know this one Father, really I do. Just give me a sec, OK?"

I avoided the sacrament for a long time. First I would use the usual excuses; *I confess to the man himself, I don't need to confess to a priest.* Then I would come up with unusual excuses; *I always mess it up, walk in on people or something, best to leave it alone.*

But after the church fire I felt distant from my faith and decided to go to confession just to talk about it with a priest. Too intimidated to go local, I went to another church for confession. The priest there told me to pray about my feelings. Well that didn't help, I already knew that.

Eventually the distance did dissolve and I figured that particular confession covered me for a bit. Years later, after living in sin with Zack, I felt I was definitely due. I decided I wasn't going to wimp out either. I was going directly to our parish priest and would do the confession face to face. There were no screens anymore like they still showed on TV, but you could choose to sit alongside the priest with a half wall between you if it made you feel more comfortable. Nope, I wasn't going to take the easy way out. I would sit directly across from my priest and tell him everything.

With weeks of mentally preparing myself, I headed to church. There were several people sitting in the pews near the confessional and I assumed they were waiting for our priest too. When he arrived he started preparing the altar and seemed to be taking his time about it. *Maybe you have to let him know that you are in church for the Reconciliation sacrament?*

I went up and told him why I was there. I also told him that I was nervous and hadn't been in a little while. He gave me a book to look over and said he would be right in.

When he entered the sin box, I waited a bit. I had been the last of the people around me to arrive and I didn't want to seem greedy. But no one got up. I kept waiting. Time was ticking away and Mass would start soon. I looked around and made eye contact with others trying to ascertain if they wanted to go first. They nodded and smiled and seemed to urge me on.

I went in and confessed my sins, all of them. And while my priest was very kind, he had A LOT to say. He talked and talked and I began to cringe as through the frosted glass of the confessional door I could see people lining up to confess. I was mortified but he had given me some things to think about and my penance didn't seem too harsh. Eventually, I walked out to face the group who were now staring at their watches. One man was standing up and leaning on his cane. *But I tried to offer to let you go first,* I wanted to shout.

I shamefacedly stumbled to a pew and began saying my prayers like the sinner I was. I thought that was the end of it. I had some more thinking to do but the sacrament was complete and I had faced my fear, it would be easier next time.

Until I left that late afternoon Mass, went to my grandmother's house for a visit, and then headed to my friend George's fortieth birthday party. Friends Shannon and Kristin met me at the door of the restaurant and told me they had saved me a seat. The seat they pointed to was directly alongside of our parish priest, the one and only. Our seats were so close it was all we could do to keep our arms and legs from smashing into each other. *George doesn't even go to church, how could this possibly happen?* My first social interaction with my priest just one hour after I had confessed to and been advised against my prior deepest, darkest secrets. Embarrassed and shocked, I stumbled for an appropriate way to handle the situation.

"Umm, can I buy you a drink, Father?"

I received the sacrament several other times in the years following that debacle but I tried to limit it to Lent if at all possible. In the year following my diagnosis, I was teaching religious education. Also in the program was a new religious education teacher with high energy and great ideas. He thought that for the start of Advent, we should gather his eighth-grade students and my seventh-grade students and use class time for Reconciliation. It would be voluntary for the kids and any student who did not wish to participate would have to suffer through a class with me instead. It was a good idea and I readily agreed. I knew that at least some of the kids wouldn't go to confession and so I did my part and prepared a class. Preparing class was easy. Sitting face to face with our priest was not. That took a lot of mental preparation and I was happy to do my part by hanging in the classroom and not in the confessional.

The plan worked great, and as expected, I was happily teaching the few kids who did not go, when the eighth-grade teacher came into the room towards the end of class time. He told me that the last student was in the confessional and why didn't we switch places so I could go to confession too?

While this made sense, we hadn't planned it and I hadn't prepared myself for this. I had prepared for class. A really, hard boring class in the hopes that the students would be more willing to participate in the sacrament in the future, if only to get a break from book work. I couldn't think fast enough to get out of the other teacher's suggestion and how would it look to the students if I simply said I didn't want to go. I was stuck. So I went.

I entered the church and since it had been at least ten months since my last confession and I had major memory issues, I nonchalantly asked one of the students who was saying her prayers the protocol. I asked her in a teacher-like kind of way.

"So, how did it go? Did you bless yourself first or start with your Act of Contrition?"

Good thing I pretended to test her, because judging by her answers, I was way off. I walked in and confessed to sometimes saying the Lord's name in vain, sometimes judging others, and sometimes missing Mass. Missing Mass was a biggie. He asked me why, what excuse could I possibly have for missing Mass? What came out of my mouth was, "Well, you see Father, I have a chronic illness that makes me terribly tired and sometimes I am just so tired that it is too hard for me to get my act together to come to Church. But that is really not an excuse as coming to Mass energizes me spiritually and so I should try harder in spite of the exhaustion that comes with this horrible, incurable disease."

What could my priest say to that? Nothing, apparently. He passed over that sin and went over all of the others in less than a minute. The Lord's Prayer was my penance and I was absolved, hopefully until Lent.

Kneeling in the church with the kids, I realized how my answer had sounded. I had used MS to get a pass for sins! Laurie was right. Without realizing it I had learned to play the MS card and was attempting to play it with God! As I herded the repentant students back to the classroom I expected another little push in the church parking lot. Just a little shove to remind me of what's what. Luckily, none came. Perhaps Jesus knew I didn't mean to do it.

But in case I was not getting the message enough with my own guilt, that night's short, sharp pain was right in the palm of my right hand. *It's just a coincidence,* I reasoned. *If He was trying to send me a reminder of the cross it would have been in both palms. He knows I feel bad about using MS as an excuse. This is just random MS pain, that's all.*

If this had been the first one I would have really freaked out, but I got these brief, sharp pains all the time. Laurie said they were some sort of short in your nerves' electrical system. I had never before gotten one in the palm of my hand however.

I tossed and turned on that quite a bit before finally falling asleep.

THE NEW WILD

It used to be that the Friday night questions were interesting, exciting even. Should I have a Kamikaze shot or just another beer? Should we close the bar or leave early, say 12:30 a.m.? Is this almost-cute guy a dork or just really sweet? Will the town mind if I use my staff key to open the library at 1:00 in the morning and use the copier to finish our concert posters? Should I ditch my friends to follow this guy I have been lusting after or play hard to get?

The most interesting Friday night question I remember was, if I see someone coming should I yell for you two or hit the horn? That one came up when my then-boyfriend and his boss broke into a house they were supposed to be done working on. They were flooring installers who had run of out carpet padding just before completing the job. They couldn't admit that however, as they had guaranteed the job would be finished by five. When the owner came to inspect their work, everything looked great and they swore the job was done. But after they gave the owner back her keys and she paid them very nicely, they raced to the carpet store to buy more supplies. That night, they didn't break in to steal anything, but to finish the job they had faked and claimed complete. I was the lookout as they crawled through a bedroom window to do the work before the tenants moved in the next morning. Those were the days.

But since MS, Friday questions are different. One of my most annoying MS symptoms was having to pee constantly, especially at night. Sometimes seven or eight trips to the bathroom were necessary, one immediately after the other, before I fell asleep. One particular Friday, I was watching a movie my mom had borrowed from the library and then shared with me. No expensive movie rental nights at my house: the library will do just fine, thank you.

I really wanted to have a cup of tea while I watched it. But that was a bad idea, and I knew it. It was eight o'clock, I'd be up all night for sure. If I had a cup of tea at that hour, there would be no end to my get out of bed, pee, flush, wash, back to bed cycle.

But I want it dammit! Is a cup of tea too much to ask? I said screw it and made the tea. Sitting back on my sofa and hitting play on the remote, I took a comforting sip, feeling like the rebel I was. That's right. A cup of tea. Boy was I having a wild Friday night.

Rebel with a cup of tea? What??? When did this happen? Can I blame this on MS too? But the truth was, MS or no MS, I had seen this coming. I think it was a mix of MS and simple growing up—for me and some of my friends, too. We were all changing. Just last year, Lynn had come to visit and I offered her a choice of beer or wine. She said she wasn't sure what she was in the mood for, she was going to think about it a while. Not wanting to be rude, I held off until she decided. An hour later, I asked again. She still hadn't decided. An hour after that I said, "Lynn, let me know if I can get you anything and I hope you don't think I'm weird but I am going to make myself some tea."

"Oh, tea would be great! Yes, let's have a cup." Lynn had often been my party buddy back in the day. What had we become? Now we stayed in and had tea. Another night she came over to play the Rolling Stones Trivial Pursuit game. To really honor our favorite band she also brought her Rolling Stones bobble heads. We held a Stones bash, even drinking our wine out of Rolling Stones mugs. She won the game but it was a pretty close match.

Later we both agreed the wine really wasn't that good. We hadn't enjoyed it at all. Was it too cheap? We used to drink cheap wine like it was water. Was it because it was in mugs instead of wine glasses, even if they did have the Stones logo on them? Perhaps we should have had tea. It had been a wild Friday night after all.

YOU SAY IT'S YOUR BIRTHDAY

It wasn't my birthday exactly; I had been a spring baby. But it was December, and 12/17 was fast approaching. One year after my diagnosis, my MS anniversary seemed a day that needed to be marked in some way.

I have since met many others with MS and almost all of them knew the exact day of their diagnosis. Cognitive difficulties or not, ask an MSer how long they have had MS and they will likely say, "I was diagnosed on 6/20/03" or "I received my diagnosis on 9/12/94." Even on their brain-foggiest days, they are rarely vague about it: I hardly ever hear people say, "I have had MS for six years" or "I think it was around May a few years ago." I almost always get a specific date.

The occasion needed something. What, though, I didn't know. I thought about standing my shot in the middle of a cupcake before I injected myself with my meds. Should I light the end on fire and sing Happy Birthday to my MS? No, that was beyond weird, even for me. Plus, I didn't think my nerves could take a dose of pink cupcake icing along with the Chinese hamster ovary cells.

Should I throw a party? I was too tired to organize a get-together and what would we do at this party? Instead of Pin the Tail on the Donkey we could play Pin the Shot on my Butt. That didn't sound like much fun.

Should I sing and dance around my living room as if it were a celebration? While accepting the diagnosis had taken some physical, logistical, medical, and emotional work, I was doing okay. I felt I had made great strides in the balancing act that was living with multiple sclerosis, but that didn't mean I wanted to throw confetti.

My body seemed to have some ideas of its own on how to honor the special day. 12/17 dawned with brain fog, body aches, and exhaustion galore, lest I forget the reason for the day's importance. As I have said, on those days there was little I could accomplish. Even with my favorite holiday approaching, I had to let go of any thoughts about accomplishing anything on this particular day.

Since I wasn't working, I was somewhat caught up in holiday preparations. Cards were mailed, decorations hung, the few presents that I was going to buy were bought, and most were wrapped. With no place I had to be from 9-5, I wasn't trying to cram all those holiday activities into the few hours in the month where I wasn't sleeping or working. And, since not working meant no income, I would be spending and shopping less.

I was inundated with chocolate chips, coconut, and graham crackers, as this was the time of year I baked a ton of my Bahama

Bars, the only thing I really knew how to make and truly made well. They were a Christmas staple in our family, and everybody loved them. It seemed I inherited the talent of baking them the best. So this year, with money tight, everyone on my list was getting Bahama Bars for Christmas. I had been baking them constantly.

There had been changes in the past year that would be visible during this Christmas. Christopher, my little brother and the driving hero who rescued me and made me laugh on this day last year, had graduated from his maritime college and was on a huge ship in the middle of the Pacific Ocean. My dad and stepmother would spend the holiday visiting my little sister Suzanne, who had settled in her own beautiful part of the country. My sister Audrey always spent Christmas with her husband and sons in Florida.

The biggest change was that this would be the first year my nephew Drew wouldn't be with us to open presents and create amusing family memories. He and his future wife had moved west and were expecting a baby in a couple of months. Drew being such a young dad was not in the plans we had for him, but we knew he would be great at it. And we were excited that there would be a new baby in the family, even if he would live far away. So it would be a quiet Christmas this year with just my mom, Laurie, and me, but it would still be my favorite holiday.

There were other major changes, of course. I now had an explanation for the craziness going on in my body, and with the explanation came treatments that I had never expected but could help slow down this particular craziness. And on the days when I felt really lousy, ached horribly, was too fatigued to even brush my teeth, or said something, really, really stupid, at least I now had an excuse.

I had discovered that while I was a cognitive mess, sometimes it wasn't totally me. The cell phone company was a good example. After three tries with the same model of phone that only worked half the time, the cell phone company finally gave me a new model of a basic flip phone that worked great. I had no problems making calls on this phone even though in the first week I brought it home I dropped it twice, once inside and once outside, and unintentionally threw it across the room. Yet when I made calls after, people could hear me just fine. So perhaps that little bit of crazy was not of my own doing—there was plenty of actual insanity in the world around me. Or maybe the aliens had decided to cut me a break.

Either way, I had developed a new lifestyle since my diagnosis that allowed for less stress and more rest. It was working, but it was still a balancing act. I needed to do better with taking care of myself, which is why I planned to serve carrots AND asparagus at Christmas dinner. And I had a ways to go in figuring out my future, but I was getting there.

My foggy brain considered these random thoughts as I sat on 12/17/10, playing FreeCell and thinking of the year that had passed and what the year ahead may bring. Perhaps not coincidentally, my MS anniversary fell on a shot day. I was pretty achy as I gathered the materials: alcohol swab, journal, two cotton balls, Aleve, glass of water, auto injector, and the shot itself. I didn't have a cupcake to place the shot in and I was kind of sick of Bahama Bars, so I just decided to do it straight up, no special shot honor today. In my shot journal I noticed it was a thigh day, the worst, the ones that hurt the most. Should I skip the thigh and move to a less obnoxious area since this was a special occasion? No, I decided. The shot was the shot and next week was Christmas. I would celebrate with a bang and do the suckiest shot on this anniversary so I could get it over with before the real holiday.

I hit the button on the auto-injector and my lower thigh exploded with greater pain than usual. My arm reacted to the pain by violently yanking the shot out of my leg, tearing the skin and dispersing incredibly expensive relapsing-remitting multiple sclerosis medication all over my coffee table. The blood gushing from the injection site was no match for the two cotton balls I had near me, and I stumbled into the bathroom to stop the bleeding and clean up.

So the anniversary shot didn't go so well. One year later and I was still wimpy about the shots. But such is life. I needed them and there were worse things in the world. I knew they were helping, so I would continue to do them.

And I don't think it was my imagination that the morning after the shot fiasco the wobbly leg on my coffee table suddenly seemed much more stable. Yes, there is power in knowing and treating. One year later, I was better and a little more stable, too.

SUCKS IS IN THE EYE OF THE BEHOLDER

Here are some of the brilliant and incredibly helpful things I learned in my first year of dealing with, getting to know, and accepting multiple sclerosis:

1. If you are on drugs when you buy it, a $399 computer can wind up costing you over $1,200.

2. Working as a survey taker earning five cents an hour may not be the best way to recoup financial loss.

3. If the theater you are hired to evaluate is more than twenty-five miles from your home and you buy outrageously expensive popcorn and soda while watching

the free movie, mystery shopping probably isn't a good plan for financial solvency either.

4. Life is too short to be miserable all the time.

5. Going to work and immediately going to bed when you get home is miserable.

6. If you don't uncap the needle first, the shot won't work and you will have to start the harebrained process all over again.

7. If you are wide awake and feel like you have been stabbed, and there are no intruders or malevolent spirits in your home, something may be medically wrong with you.

8. If you are so clumsy that the people dearest to you have taken to calling you "Grace" ironically, you may be able to blame it on a disease.

9. If you happen to be naked except for a fuzzy blue bathrobe when there is a knock on your door, it is a good idea to look out the window before opening it in case someone named Bootsie is on the other side.

10. MS sucks.

As Dr. M told me on the first day I met her, MS sucks. But so do a lot of things in life. Running out of toilet paper when you really need it sucks. Ruining your beautiful new manicure twenty minutes after the nail salon closes because you dropped your keys on the ground and you scraped the hell out of your index finger when you bent down to pick them up sucks. Having a tree fall on your new car during a freak early winter windstorm while you are at the post office mailing Christmas presents sucks. (Scene from another crazy Christmas but I still love the holiday!)

In the scheme of varying degrees of things that suck, MS is definitely up there on the list. And when you are diagnosed with a chronic illness such as multiple sclerosis, you become filled with horribly negative emotions such as terror, anger, bitterness, resentment, worry, sadness, and a whole list of feelings that can destroy you. Those depressing emotions just hang around inside you and form a force field with the evil little army of antibodies determined to bring you down. You must beat these little suckers up! Don't let them win!

These negative pieces of emotion are battling against keeping you happy and sane. But that's not all, folks! With MS, you also get strange things going on in your body that can run the gamut from annoying, to painful, to absolutely debilitating. You have this crappy stuff in your body attacking crucial myelin you didn't even know existed before your diagnosis, and you're also dealing with the emotion of having the disease. You have got to get those bad emotions out of your body and fast! Crying is a good way to release these emotions and it definitely helps. I know I have gone through boxes and boxes of tissues this past year.

But laughter is also a legitimate way to release negative energy. And, I have learned, laughter is more fun. I cried plenty when I found out I had MS, but then I decided I needed to laugh if I was to survive and thrive. Maybe my laughter only lasted for a short time, but isn't it better to feel good, even briefly, than to get dragged down by suffering? A smile is like a tiny defense field against all that dark icky stuff hanging around in you. A gut-splitting howl of laughter is like a full-scale attack on the little fort of destructive energy in your body. More laughs, and they're screaming, "Retreat! Run for cover! This madwoman has a giggle stick and she is trying to beat the crap out of us with it!" Come to think of it, I have gone through boxes of tissues with tears of laughter, too. Kleenex must love me!

What I've learned is that even things that are completely rotten can be turned inside out. Here's some of the other stuff I learned during this journey, lessons that didn't actually suck.

1. If your dad has good taste in music, having him play Morgan Freeman to your Jessica Tandy in your own upside-down version of *Driving Miss Daisy* may not be a bad thing. But if English is his second language, make sure you bring ear plugs.

2. A dysfunctional relationship with your animated exercise video-gaming system is better than no relationship at all.

3. There comes a time when your little brother is no longer your little brother even though he is still your little brother. I mean, he will always be your little brother. But there may be times when he is actually your hero, the guy you go to for help, even though you're the older sister and you feel like you should be helping him. And even though you may need his help, you can always remind him he's your little brother and you get to boss him around because you're the big sister. And that is a comforting thing.

4. If #3 is confusing perhaps it is a bad brain fog day and you need a nap. I know I do … Despite what every two-year-old on the planet will tell you, naps rock.

5. Sometimes your mom's shoes don't need to actually fit in order to fit just right.

6. Chinese hamsters are our friends. If they want to give us their ovary cells for medicine, we should just be grateful.

7. Speaking of friends, if you are confused by your MS, imagine how confused your friends must be. Try to give them a break if they say something clueless. Especially if they have a sense of humor. Or chocolate.

8. When you find yourself shuffling and crying through Kmart, your tears are probably about something bigger than the blue light special. You may need to stop, breathe, and figure out what that is ... And when you figure it out, you might stop crying.

9. Yes, quitting your job is super scary. Accepting MS is super-duper scary. Abandoned string cheese is not scary at all.

10. It's true. MS positively, without a doubt, sucks. But on many levels, how you handle that fact can affect the level of suckiness in your life. Or, as I like to say, how you deal can help how you feel.

Let's face it, I've been fortunate thus far with my diagnosis and symptoms. I know many people with my condition who have been through much worse, but when talking together and recounting our stories, if we can find common ground on a little MS madness, laughing together feels like some good, kick butt medicine. It is okay to be really, really mad at this obnoxious, damaging, and weird disease. And it is okay to cry when overwhelmed. But I have learned that laughing helps too, and laughing leaves me with a smile and positive energy in which to move forward. And moving forward is something I insist on. It is something you should insist on as well.

MS potentially can mean the end of some things for you. But if you can find a way to tame the bad emotions that come with it, it doesn't have to stop you. If you dig deep down and find what truly inspires you, you can do anything you really want to. You can still dream anything you want to. You may have to adjust your dreams and it doesn't hurt to be realistic about them.

Allow me to offer you a personal illustration. It has always been my dream to be an amazing rock star, with the vocal styling of, say, Stevie Nicks or Chrissie Hynde. But since that damn MS, my vocal chords just aren't good enough. (OK, in reality, I have had a terrible singing voice ever since I was a kid, but that doesn't mean I can't blame it on MS if I want to!)

So maybe that is not the best dream for me to have. But our dreams are ours alone and it doesn't matter what is going on with your body; if you really want it, you can achieve it. It may be a lot tougher than it was before. And you may have to change your dream and rest a bit more than expected on the path to achieving it. Maybe you have to make a pit stop in the middle of your dream to administer one of your dreaded shots, drink some water, hit the bathroom, or do your physical therapy. But if it is in your heart, you can do it.

The truth is, life is going to constantly throw some sucky stuff your way. How you survive the suckiness depends on you and you alone. Allow a Cape Cod girl and the granddaughter of fishermen to tell you a fish story about survival, a true fish story more unbelievable than all other fish stories. While fishing for halibut in the late 1800s, a Gloucester dory man named Howard Blackburn was caught in an unexpected, severe winter storm. His dory was blown out of sight of the schooner he was fishing on, the cruelest of the cruel when it comes to things that suck. Then, in the commotion of the storm he lost his mittens overboard. I think we can all agree that *really* sucks. How much suckiness should one person be forced to endure?

Howard refused to lie down and give up; he chose to survive. The only thing he could think to do to survive was to row. So row he did. He rowed for several days without food, water, or sleep. He rowed with the added weight of his crewmen who had frozen to death shortly after they were lost and whom Howard insisted on bringing home for a proper burial. Knowing it wouldn't take long for his limbs to freeze, Howard kept his fingers curved around the oars so that they would freeze in the rowing position. When he finally made it to land five days later, rowing the entire way, doctors discovered frostbite had claimed all of his fingers, several toes and part of both of his thumbs. He was told his sailing days were over.

Howard decided a little thing like no fingers and hardly any thumbs was not going to stop him. He chose to keep sailing and went on to set records for the fastest solo sailing trips across the Atlantic, captaining a small dory to do so. When he chose to stop sailing, he used the money he made from setting records to buy a small tavern. I like to picture Howard behind the bar of the tavern, a tankard of ale in front of him, telling his story, perhaps (unnecessarily) embellishing it, as fishermen are known to do. I just know Howard was laughing while he told the tale …

Howard chose survival. But it was more than surviving his journey home in the storm; he wanted to live well once he got there, too. When he achieved that, he dreamed of proving to people that his disability wouldn't stop him. When he achieved that, he dreamed of setting records. And when he had done that, he opened a bar where people paid him for drinks and to hear his story over and over again. Howard survived, lived well despite a serious disability, and lived out his dreams. Howard Blackburn is my hero!

So maybe I gave up on my dream to become a great singer (like in sixth grade) and am way too tired to row across the Atlantic (luckily we have airplanes now). Today my dream is to live well and make my living as a published writer. I can find the strength to do that. So I have written a book. Will it be successful? It will if you buy it and tell your friends and family to buy it too. (Subliminal message and subtle play of the MS card here—buy, buy, buy.) I wrote this book with my heart, my sense of humor, and my dreams; not with my aches, my pains, my miserable bladder, my brain fog, or my fatigue. With a smile on my face. Luckily, I had my $399 laptop that actually cost $1,200 to help me.

The main thing I have learned since my diagnosis is that how you deal with the diagnosis can have everything to do with how you survive your diagnosis, and change your life. I choose to use the strength of my funny bone to beat the crap out of multiple sclerosis whenever possible. And, I swear, I feel much better for it. I feel so good, perhaps I will row across the Atlantic. Tomorrow. Right now, I will listen to some jokes and maybe take a nap.

Oh, and I forgot something crucial that I learned on my MS journey. Most important of all, we should eat our vegetables. Even if they do, well, you know, suck.

Acknowledgments

It takes a lifetime of support and a whole lot of work to pull a book together. I am incredibly grateful to the many people who have guided me on this journey both before this book and after, and before multiple sclerosis and after. Family, new friends, old friends, I thank and cherish you all.

Specifically I would like to mention the Cape Cod Writer's Center for getting me started and the awesome folks at SDP Publishing for pulling it all together. Lisa—you're a rock! Aileen—you're a rock star! I would also like to recognize the many early readers who chuckled at this story and then apologized, thinking it was inappropriate to do so. Forgive me if I leave anyone out (or blame it on MS, I certainly do) but some of these fantastic folks are Ernie, Sheryl, Paul, Nicola, Gail, Laura, Marie, Nancy, Barbara #1, Barbara #2, Jerri, Joan, Anita, Nikole, Pat, and Carol. Thank you to Michael for all the heavy web lifting and for keeping me from pulling my hair out.

I am indebted to Samantha, Dottie (I miss you), Shannon, Christine, Monika, and Dora for all of their encouragement. Yes, kids, Dora the Explorer is alive and well and lives in Massachusetts—*vamanos*! And I am blessed to have my Boston Bruins fairy godmother Kristin, and my Rolling Stones fairy godmother Lynn. Thank you for getting me out of the house when I was about to crack and no lame ear plugs were needed! Thank you to Serena and Heather for their giggles, lifelong friendship, and providing cigarettes when I needed them even though I am not really a smoker.

Thank you to my dad for being my dad, my personal chauffeur for dreaded city appointments, and for having excellent taste in music. And even though my mom has lousy taste in music, I thank her for all of her love, guidance, and support in just about everything. She is the coolest of the cool when it comes to being a mom. She is like the incarnation of Keith Richards, Fonzie, and Elvis of moms!

Most of all, thank you to God who sent all these amazing and wonderful people my way, and for giving each of us a sense of humor in the first place!

About the Author

Yvonne deSousa has worked as a street sweeper, a shell seller, a babysitter, a candy peddler, and a guest house manager, all before the age of sixteen. Later on she worked as a waitress, sales clerk, library assistant, victim's advocate, and at the front desk of a doctor's office.

Two years before Yvonne's diagnosis of multiple sclerosis, a relative volunteered her to write an article for a local newspaper. Little did she know it was the beginning of a writing career. When MS threatened to turn her into a lunatic, she started writing more frequently, eventually publishing her work in newspapers, an online digest, and in *Chicken Soup for the Soul: Finding My Faith*. She writes a regular blog on www.yvonnedesousa.com and presents programs designed to help others use humor to help cope with chronic illness.

Yvonne enjoys writing, laughing, and resting.

MS Madness
A "Giggle More, Cry Less" Story of Mulitple Sclerosis

Author: **Yvonne deSousa**
Website: yvonnedesousa.com
Publisher: SDP Publishing

Available in print and ebook formats on:
Amazon
BarnesAndNoble.com
SDPPublishing.com

www.SDPPublishing.com
Contact us at: info@SDPPublishing.com

CPSIA information can be obtained at www.ICGtesting.com
Printed in the USA
BVOW08s0854170214

345037BV00003B/4/P